United States Congress, U.S. Dept. of the Treasury, House
Committee on Banking and Currency

Resumption of Speciel Payments

Notes of a conference between the Committee on banking and currency

of the House of representatives and the Hon. John Sherman, secretary of

the Treasury, April 1st and 4th, 1878

United States Congress, U.S. Dept. of the Treasury, House Committee on Banking and Currency

Resumption of Speciel Payments
Notes of a conference between the Committee on banking and currency of the House of representatives and the Hon. John Sherman, secretary of the Treasury, April 1st and 4th, 1878

ISBN/EAN: 9783337400156

Printed in Europe, USA, Canada, Australia, Japan

Cover: Foto ©Suzi / pixelio.de

More available books at **www.hansebooks.com**

RESUMPTION OF SPECIE PAYMENTS.

NOTES OF A CONFERENCE

BETWEEN THE

COMMITTEE ON BANKING AND CURRENCY

OF THE

HOUSE OF REPRESENTATIVES

AND THE

HON. JOHN SHERMAN, SECRETARY OF THE TREASURY,

APRIL 1ST AND 4TH, 1878.

MEMBERS OF THE COMMITTEE:

HON. A. H. BUCKNER, Chairman.

MESSRS. THOMAS EWING, AUGUSTUS A. HARDENBERGH, JESSE J. YEATES, WILLIAM HARTZELL, HIRAM P. BELL, E. KIRKE HART, BENJ. T. EAMES, S. B. CHITTENDEN, GREENBURY L. FORT, AND WILLIAM A. PHILLIPS.

WASHINGTON:
GOVERNMENT PRINTING OFFICE.
APRIL, 1878.

COMMITTEE ON BANKING AND CURRENCY,
HOUSE OF REPRESENTATIVES,
Washington, April 1, 1878.

Present, Mr. Buckner, chairman;
Messrs. Ewing, Hardenbergh, Hartzell, Bell, Eames, Chittenden, Fort, and Phillips;
The Hon. John Sherman, Secretary of the Treasury.

The chairman read to the Secretary a copy of the letter sent to him on the 28th ultimo, in which were stated the several points upon which the committee wished to be informed at the conference set for to-day. The first was a statement showing the actual amount of gold and silver coin and bullion belonging to or in the custody of the Treasury Department on the 28th of March, where located, and what deductions were to be made from it on account of actual existing demands against it.

Secretary SHERMAN. I can give you a statement up to the 28th of February, 1878. I am not able now to give you the statement for the month of March, but can do it to-morrow or next day, and I will probably attach it to my answer. This, however, is the general result of the statement. We have at the Treasury, the different subtreasuries, assay-offices, and depositories:

In gold coin	$113,351,709
In gold bullion	7,937,300
In subsidiary silver coin	5,675,494
And in silver bullion	2,955,577

(See Appendix No. 3.)

I have also got the comparative debt statement, but I think I had better not put it in now, because I will have the complete statement made to day. This being the first of the month, it could not be made up until to-day. (See Appendix No. 5.)

The CHAIRMAN. The next point called for by the committee is a statement of gold and silver coin and bullion in the Treasury, less the items deducted in your statement made before the Senate Finance Committee, from 1865 to 1877, inclusive.

Secretary SHERMAN. The Treasurer has tried to give that statement, as far as he can, but he could not give it complete, except as to the statement made on the 1st of February, 1877. In this statement he says this:

The committee, in their inquiry No. 2, asked for a statement similar to the above, for each year from 1865. It has been found impracticable to comply, as to the years from 1865 to 1876, in the short time allowed, on account of the form in which reports from assistant treasurers and mints and assay offices were made prior to 1877. In fact, to make the statement as requested would necessitate correspondence with all the above offices.

I told him that as this statement gives you the items a year ago, and as you have also that statement for this year, that was all you would probably want. The amount of gold and silver available on the 1st of

February, 1877, was $11,936,771, after making the same deductions as were made in the table given to the Finance Committee, on page 4. This table (Appendix No. 2) contrasting with that table will show the condition of the Treasury as to gold and silver then and on the 1st of February of this year. The amount a year ago was $11,938,771, and the amount on the 1st of February this year was $71,775,860, making the increase of gold and silver available between the 1st of February, 1878 and the 1st of February, 1877, $59,839,089.

This statement (handing it to the committee) will give you the amount in silver coin, in silver bullion, in gold coin, &c.

There was another fact which I thought the committee would desire to have in this connection. I thought that the committee would want to know the distribution of this money on the 28th of March, 1878. We had in gold coin and standard silver dollars $114,666,958; in fractional silver coin $5,736,639; and in gold and silver bullion $13,664,914. The amount of silver standard dollars included in this is estimated at $454,711. (See Appendix No. 4.)

The CHAIRMAN. The third inquiry is the amount of bonds sold up to February 1, 1878, and not paid for.

Secretary SHERMAN. If that question means simply to inquire as to the amount of bonds not paid for at that date, my answer is that they are all paid for. There are no bonds issued unless they are paid for; but I suppose that what the committee means by this question is to ascertain the amount of bonds actually sold for resumption purposes, and also for refunding purpose. I have the distribution here; but in direct answer to the question it will be perhaps sufficient for me to say that there are no bonds which have not been paid for. We take subscriptions, but never issue the bonds until we get the money. An arrangement has been made with the Bank of Commerce, in New York, by which we allow that bank to collect currency and coin drafts for bonds, and when the coin is paid into the Treasury the bonds are sent to the person. The actual amount of bonds sold under the resumption act and under the refunding act is as follows:

Under the resumption act—

5 per cent. bonds of 1881	$17,494,350
4½ per cent. bonds of 1891	15,000,000
4 per cent. bonds of 1907	25,000,000
Total	57,494,350

The bonds issued on account of refunding are as follows:

5 per cent. bonds of 1881	$490,000,000
4½ per cent. bonds of 1891	185,000,000
4 per cent. bonds of 1907	55,000,000
Total	730,796,200

Which last sum added to the $57,494,350 on account of resumption makes the total $788,290,550.

I ought to say that the proceeds of all the bonds that were sold under the refunding act were applied to the payment of an equal amount of 5·20 bonds bearing 6 per cent. interest.

The CHAIRMAN. These bonds were sold at par, were they not?

Secretary SHERMAN. Yes, sir; par in coin. We paid out of the Treasury one-half of 1 per cent. for commissions and expenses.

The CHAIRMAN. The fourth inquiry is as to the usual amount of annual coin liabilities of the government, stating separately the liabilities for interest, sinking-fund, foreign service, &c.

Secretary SHERMAN. I have this for last year. It is as follows:

Coin interest paid during fiscal year 1877	$92,883,431 27
Amount applied to the sinking-fund during fiscal year 1877	447,500 00
Amount paid for diplomatic service during fiscal year 1877	755,286 06
Amount paid for foreign naval service during fiscal year 1877	2,224,124 49
Amount of customs refunds during fiscal year 1877	5,247,800 65
Amount expended for refunding national debt, parting and refining bullion, &c., during fiscal year 1877	901,927 30
Total	102,460,069 77

You are aware that under the law importers very often deposit money in advance of their entries, and then, when their entries are liquidated, the excess is returned to them. That system is adopted in order to enable them to get their goods quickly. Also in some cases where disputes arise as to the amount of duties, if the duties are paid in excess, the excess is refunded. These refunds are in the ordinary current course of business.

The CHAIRMAN. This total of $102,460.09 is the coin payments for the last fiscal year?

Secretary SHERMAN. Yes, sir; divided up in the way I have stated.

The CHAIRMAN. The fifth question which the committee desired you to answer, is the amount of fractional currency redeemed and carried to the account of the sinking fund, and what applications of coin, if any, have been made on account of the sinking fund during the current fiscal year.

Secretary SHERMAN. The answer to that is:

The amount of fractional currency applied to the sinking fund in 1876 was $7,062,142.09, and in 1877, $14,043,458.05. So far in this fiscal year the redemptions of fractional currency amount to $3,382,621.45, making a total of $24,488,2.1.59 applied to that fund. No coin applications have been made to the sinking fund during the current fiscal year, except the redemptions of bonds heretofore called, amounting to $67,700.

Some cases occurred where bonds were sent on by parties by mistake, and we redeemed them; and they were put into the sinking fund. After that we adopted the habit of returning bonds that were sent by mistake.

The CHAIRMAN. The next question is, what is meant by balances in the sinking-fund accounts? Of what items are those balances made up?

Secretary SHERMAN. It is very natural for any person, lawyer or business man, to be misled by the use of the word "balance" in these sinking-fund accounts. A balance may not be a balance of money in hand; and, in this particular case, the word "balance" means either an amount of the sinking fund which has not been made good by the purchase of bonds, or an excess of the amount required by law. These are called balances, and this table on page 18 of the Finance Report shows very fully how the sinking fund is made up, and of what items it is composed. This table goes back to 1869, and shows at the end of that fiscal year a balance to new account; that is, the balance to new account is a balance in this case of an amount paid—more than the law required—into the sinking fund, and therefore it is put to the credit of the sinking-fund for the next year.

Then, the next year, they had not bought quite as many bonds for the sinking fund as the sinking-fund law required, and so there was a balance of $1,254,000 which was carried to the credit of the sinking fund to be made up the next year, and so on. These balances continued, amounting to somewhere between half a million and a million and a half of dollars. Sometimes they would be on the one side and sometimes on the other, and they were carried forward until 1873 or 1874, when, after the panic, the revenues fell off, and they failed to make good the sinking fund. The amount of deficit in making good the sinking fund in 1874 was stated at $16,305,000. Mr. Bristow, I am told, declined to carry forward this balance to the next year because it was apparent that, from the condition of the finances, he would not be able to make good that balance in addition to the sinking fund for the next year, and therefore the balance was dropped. It represents simply the amount which the government failed to apply to the sinking fund. Instead of carrying it forward in his accounts, the Secretary dropped it. That is what I did last year, and what Mr. Morrill had done. We did not undertake to carry forward the deficiency in one year to swell the sinking fund for the next year.

Mr. BELL. Then this term "balance" applied to the sinking fund indicates either the excess or the deficit in the sinking fund for the year?

Secretary SHERMAN. That is all. At first the balances were carried forward and were made good the next year, because they did not amount to much; but when the deficit became so great, and when it became apparent that it could not be made good, the Secretary just dropped it. Now, last year we were deficient in the sinking fund $9,235,000, simply because we could not, out of the surplus revenue, make good that fund.

The CHAIRMAN. On the whole, have not the deficiencies in the sinking-fund account been more than made good since the passage of the act?

Secretary SHERMAN. Yes. You will find a statement of that in Mr. Morrill's report. The sinking fund was never kept as an account in the Treasury Department until after the refunding act of 1870. A section in the refunding act provided for the stating of the account of the sinking fund, and then it was first commenced. Up to that time a statement was made showing how far the sinking fund had been kept under the act of February, 1862, and it was found that by the application of the surplus revenue to the payment of the debt, the stipulations of the sinking fund act had been largely exceeded, to the amount of $200,000,000. Now the sinking-fund account is regularly kept, and the exact statement of it is shown by Mr. Morrill's reports and also by my annual reports.

The CHAIRMAN. Have you the report of the examiners at the subtreasury office, New York, as to the coin there?

Secretary SHERMAN. Yes, sir; I have the preliminary report of Mr. E. O. Graves, which is as follows:

TREASURY OF THE UNITED STATES,
Washington, March 29, 1878.

SIR: I have the honor to submit a preliminary report upon the examination of the office of the assistant treasurer of the United States in New York, recently made under my direction in pursuance of the instructions given in your letter of the 11th instant. The funds found in the possession of that office at the close of business on the 12th instant, at which time I took charge (exclusive of currency and coupons in process of redemption and not charged to the cash), were as follows, the coin being verified by weight and the notes, currency, and securities by actual count and examination of each individual obligation:

Gold coin	$100,051,280 00
Gold bars	3,367,713 26
Coin checks, paid on March 12, 1878, but not charged up	1,039,114 78
Silver coin	1,396,436 28
Coin certificates	3,197,900 00
United States notes	32,614,479 00
National currency	428,711 00
Fractional currency and minor coin	194,058 92

Redeemed legal-tender certificates of deposit, June 8, 1872	$3,335,000 00
Coin coupons	8,368 10
Coupons of District of Columbia bonds	110 41
Treasurer's checks for registered interest on District of Columbia bonds	273 75
Redeemed call bonds and interest	2,013 48
Treasurer's coin quarterly-interest checks:	
Funded loan of 1881	48,168 03
Funded loan of 1891	832,383 02
Funded loan of 1907	3,603 50
Receipts for advances on salaries of employés	2,421 00
Cash for petty expenses in cashier's hands	15 00
Seven-thirty notes purchased, being balance of amount of counterfeit 7-30 notes purchased, and for which judgment has been obtained in favor of the United States	8,750 31
Total	146,560,829 84
Total as shown by assistant treasurer'r report of March 12, 1878.	146,566,996 35
Deficit	6,166 51

Only $1,777.51 of the deficit arose in the seven and one-half years during which the present incumbent has held the office of assistant treasurer, and of that amount $1,500 is due to a single shortage discovered in a package of notes received from a bank in payment of a draft, but which the bank refused to make good. This leaves a deficit from all other causes during the present assistant treasurer's incumbency of but $277.51; a most remarkable record considering the vast amount of money which has passed through his hands. The items composing the entire deficit will be explained in full in my final report.

Very respectfully, your obedient servant,

E. O. GRAVES.

To Hon. JOHN SHERMAN,
   Secretary of the Treasury.

The items of this deficit had been reported and known at the department, so that there was no actual variation between the statement as made by the assistant treasurer and the actual count. Perhaps I ought to say that this count occurred also here in Washington in July last, at the time that Mr. Gilfillan took possession of the Treasurer's Office. Every item and paper was counted before he gave his receipt for the money, and everything was found to be correct, except a small item of $1,831, of which we have a full account.

Mr. CHITTENDEN. I have prepared four questions in the interest of those whom I represent, to which I should like to have your answer:

First. With silver dollars and silver certificates full legal tender for all debts, including the customs and the public debt, is not gold practically demonetized; and how will you renew your supplies, or prevent its exclusive use as merchandise in foreign commerce?

Second. Is there no danger that the national banks, in taking care of themselves, will hoard greenbacks enough to exhaust your gold reserves when the day for resumption comes?

Third. Is it not probable that, before you have coined 100,000,000 of the new silver dollars, with greater activity in foreign trade, they will be exported at their bullion value to settle trade balances, and with what effect upon the price of silver bullion?

Fourth. Does not your success in resuming coin payments with our so-called double standard depend absolutely upon an advance in the price of silver bullion in London to about 59 pence sterling per ounce?

I have not spoken with any member of the committee in framing these questions. They were framed at my own table, and I am influenced only by my correspondence and by questions asked of me by those whom I represent.

Secretary SHERMAN. I would a great deal rather, in this connection, give the committee the facts and let the committee draw its own inferences, than attempt to give my own opinions. But I have no objections to answering any of those questions. I think that a certain amount of silver dollars issued will not have the effect which Mr. Chittenden thinks. I believe we can maintain at par in gold a certain amount of silver dollars; precisely what amount I would not like to say, because that is a question of opinion. But I have the idea that we can maintain at par in gold no less than $50,000,000; perhaps more—say from $50,000,000 to $100,000,000; but whenever those silver dollars become so abundant and so burdensome that the people would not have them and would not take them, and that they would not circulate, then undoubtedly they would gradually sink to the value of the bullion in them. That is my opinion, but I do not think it wise for either this committee or myself to discuss this question much, because the silver bill is a law, and, whatever we may think of its effects, the public mind will not be satisfied until that law is fairly tried. The effect of the silver bill is not going to be very rapid, nor will the fall in silver be anything like so rapid as is probably feared, and long before the silver dollar can sink to the value of silver bullion, Congress will undoubtedly correct the law if it were to have that effect. If, on the other hand, it should have the effect, which is anticipated, of raising the mass of silver up to the standard of gold, then Mr. Chittenden need not be afraid. Therefore, I say that I do not think I ought to give my opinion further on that subject. I have not changed my mind about the silver bill, although the newspapers say that I have. I think that (as a matter of policy) the silver bill, which makes silver available to pay bonds issued by the United States either before or after the refunding or resumption acts, is not good policy. I have stated that over and over again publicly, and I do not deny it. But the silver bill is the law. We are not infallible. It cannot operate quickly in that way, and therefore we had better give it the full benefit of an experiment, in the certainty that, if Congress finds that it has the effect which is now anticipated, Congress can at any moment stop the issue of silver dollars. I think that that is as far as I ought to answer these questions.

Mr. CHITTENDEN. It is not my object to embarrass the Secretary in any way in these questions.

The CHAIRMAN. The Secretary is of the opinion that "Sufficient to the day is the evil thereof;" that we will take care of the present, and let the future take care of itself.

Secretary SHERMAN. If you allow me, I can now, in connection with your question in regard to my opinion as to the practicability of resumption, and especially in regard to an interview published in the newspapers between Mr. Ewing and bankers in New York, give you my opinion. I have read that interview with a great deal of attention, because I know many of the gentlemen who took part in it.

The CHAIRMAN. It is proper for me on the part of the committee to say that it was not intended that that interview should be made public; but the report of it was surreptitiously obtained in some way.

Secretary SHERMAN. I do not think there was the slightest objection to publishing it.

The CHAIRMAN. Only probably on account of confidential relations.

Mr. EWING. We told those gentlemen at the conference that we had our secretary for the purpose of taking down their statements, not with a view to publishing them, but merely for the information of the committee, and the committee feels exceedingly annoyed about the publication, because it seems like a violation of that understanding; but the paper was surreptitiously obtained, and the committee does not feel at fault about it.

Mr. CHITTENDEN. Special pains were taken at New York to exclude newspaper reporters.

Secretary SHERMAN. It is pretty hard to exclude newspaper reporters; but I think it was right enough to have that conference published. It presents the opinions of very intelligent gentlemen, whose business it is to be familiar with the subject, and their opinions are entitled to full weight. I can only give you my general reply to them.

My reply would be about this: These gentlemen assume three propositions. First, that we cannot sell enough 4 per cent. bonds to prepare for resumption; second, that the national banks can throw upon the government the burden of resumption of bank-notes as well as of United States notes; third, that resumption requires the resumption and cancellation, without power of reissue, of United States notes below $300,000,000. To these I answer, that I believe that, with such auxiliary legislation as is pending in both houses, we can sell enough 4 per cent. bonds to prepare for resumption; but, if I am mistaken in this, we can sell either 4½ or 5 per cent. bonds, which they admit will command gold, silver, and bank-notes, to maintain resumption. Some of these gentlemen have proposed to me that, if I sell them 4½ per cent. bonds at par in coin, they will guarantee enough coin for resumption; and I have some better offers from other banks and bankers, so that, on this point, it is only a question of rate of interest on bonds. When it becomes clear that money cannot be had for 4 per cent., it is time enough to pay 4½. The silver bill has crippled my power to sell 4 per cent. bonds, but a wise savings bill, that will enable me to deal directly with the people, would go far to repair this. Upon the second point: It may as well be understood that the national banks cannot throw upon the government the burden of redeeming their notes. The attempt would be suicide. They are bound to redeem their notes on demand at the Treasury with United States notes or coin, and to maintain in their vaults very large reserves of United States notes. Any effort of theirs to force the redemption of their reserves of United States notes in coin would at once cause the government to withdraw all government deposits from them, to present all bank-notes held or received by the government for redemption, and, if need be, to exchange United States notes for bank-notes.

Such a struggle as these gentlemen contemplate would end in their losing their power to issue circulating notes at all. Their talk about forming a line to break the government is not discreet and is not dangerous. I am more concerned about what you will do than about what they will do. The United States Government already holds a larger cash reserve for the redemption of its notes in proportion to demand liabilities than any bank represented by these gentlemen, and it has power to increase it. Our certificates of deposit—the most dangerous form of liabilities—are secured, dollar for dollar, by coin or United States notes actually in hand, while the banks owe over $600,000,000 to depositors, the great body of which is represented by notes and bills discounted. The only demand liability we owe not covered by actual cash on hand is the United States notes, and of these $70,000,000 are in our vaults, and $70,000,000 more the banks are bound to retain in their reserves. With a coin reserve of $100,000,000 to $150,000,000, the redemption of $300,000,000 of United States notes would be easy, and that reserve could not be diminished to any considerable extent by the banks, or any combination of banks, without a continuous draft upon the banks to make it good.   We can rely upon the intelligent self-interest of the banks to prevent such a struggle.   Nothing could provoke it more quickly than threats by bank officers, and if such a struggle comes, the government, with its reserve, with ample revenue, and the power to sell bonds, can easily maintain resumption, without fear of a line of bank cashiers anxious to break the Treasury or to force high rates of interest.

On the last point: The power to reissue is plainly given by section 3579, Revised Statutes, and is not cut off any more by the notes coming into the Treasury in exchange for coin than in payment of a tax.   Even if the Supreme Court hold them as no longer a full legal tender, they are as much so as a bank-note.   If the choice must be made between the two, the common interest would decide in favor of the United States note.   I believe they both ought to circulate and both be at par with coin.   But nothing is so discouraging in the progress of resumption as for national banks to shrink from their share of the burden, or to make threats such as are stated by some of these gentlemen; and nothing is so injurious to the banking system, or will precipitate its overthrow more certainly, than a popular conviction that the banks are endeavoring to embarrass the government in maintaining resumption.

Mr. CHITTENDEN.   I did not hear anything on the part of those gentlemen with whom we conversed at the sub-treasury in the form of a threat, and I appeal to Mr. Ewing to confirm my impression.   There was nothing of that kind intended, I am sure.   These gentlemen simply expressed the opinion that in an attempt to resume with any stock of gold that you were likely to have, the gold would be transferred to the banks naturally.

Mr. EWING.   That was it.

Mr. CHITTENDEN.   There was nothing like a threat?

Mr. EWING.   No; on the contrary, there was a great desire manifested on the part of the bankers to make resumption safe.

Secretary SHERMAN.   I have written propositions from these gentlemen, and from Mr. Coe himself, that if I will give them 4½ per cent. bonds instead of 4 per cents., they will guarantee resumption.   The trouble is this, that when I am trying to sell bonds at 4 per cent., they say I am acting both as a politician and as a financier.   I suppose they mean that as a politician I am desirous to have the interest low, and that as a financier I am indifferent to the rate.   I simply say that as soon as I cannot sell 4 per cent. bonds to the people, I know I can sell 4½ per cents. to the banks; and in that way, if in no other, we can get enough gold to insure and to maintain resumption.   To that I pledge my opinion and my earnest conviction.

Now, in regard to the reserve that is necessary, there is a difference of opinion.   I would like to have so strong a reserve that there would be no question of our ability to resume, and I think (as I stated to the Committee on Finance of the Senate) that if I can have a reserve of one hundred and thirty millions; or, in other words, if I can increase my present reserve about fifty millions, I do not see how it is possible to prevent us from resuming.   If it were known to-day that it was certain, I should have such a reserve by the first of January, and if it were certain that Congress would be willing to stand by the experiment of resumption, we would have resumption at once.

Mr. EWING.   Neither of which can be made certain.

Secretary SHERMAN.   Yes; if I could sell the bonds and get the reserve, the thing would be made certain in 24 hours.

Mr. Ewing. Where do you suppose you could get so large a sum of metal?

Secretary Sherman. We produce bullion enough in this country. If I had this year's production of gold and silver (and I could very easily get it by selling bonds) I would have reserve enough.

Mr. Ewing. Would you get any part of it abroad?

Secretary Sherman. Yes; some from abroad.

Mr. Phillips. In your statement to the Senate committee as published, I understand you to say that there has been no increase of coin in the Treasury during the most of this year. Am I correct that you have not increased your coin through the months of January, February or March?

Secretary Sherman. No, sir. That is, we have not increased the coin belonging to the government, but the banks have increased on their deposits.

Mr. Phillips. Is not the depreciated price of gold owing to the fact that the banks have taken it?

Secretary Sherman. No, sir; but simply because we went out of the market for the gold.

Mr. Phillips. You have stated that you have not increased the volume of gold in the Treasury during this year.

Secretary Sherman. No, sir; because we have not sold any bonds.

Mr. Phillips. Was the attempt made to sell bonds, and were you unable to do so?

Secretary Sherman. I have tried very hard to sell them and I could sell at a higher rate of interest. Let me explain that. The reason why I cannot sell bonds, is because they have got the impression in Europe that this silver bill is going to derange matters, and that belief brought back upon us (as these gentlemen say) seventy-five millions of bonds. As a matter of course, they came into competition with the Secretary in selling bonds; and as long as they had their bonds to sell, under a scaring market, I could not sell bonds unless the rate of interest was raised.

Mr. Phillips. Then you cannot resume safely unless you can sell bonds at a higher rate of interest?

Secretary Sherman. I do not say that. I think I can. If you pass a bill to enable me to sell directly to the people I think I can sell 4 per cent. bonds.

Mr. Phillips. How about 3.65 bonds?

Secretary Sherman. I cannot sell them.

The Chairman. I do not see how that is to aid you in resumption; because in selling bonds to the people you must sell them for greenbacks.

Secretary Sherman. Yes, sir.

The Chairman. The effect of all that is to equalize greenbacks with gold. Is that the theory?

Secretary Sherman. Partly that, and partly because with greenbacks we can buy gold or anything else. The law authorizes me to buy or to sell gold, and as a matter of course I can buy gold at the market price.

The Chairman. If the people paid greenbacks for 4 per cent. bonds, then you could sell these greenbacks for gold.

Secretary Sherman. Yes, sir.

Mr. Bell. You mentioned that the interest paid in coin was about ninety-two millions a year; have you any means of ascertaining what proportion of that amount is paid abroad.

Secretary Sherman. It is very difficult to state that. The interest is all paid to agents here, and we cannot distinguish the amount of interest that is paid to bondholders here, from the amount that is paid abroad. The best estimate that I can form is that the amount of bonds held abroad is about six hundred million dollars; but there is a difference of opinion about that. I think that that is pretty near the thing.

Mr. EAMES. I desire to present to the committee, in the presence of the Secretary of the Treasury, a consideration which, I think, is important in determining the question whether the government can resume or not in January, 1879. There is now outstanding about three hundred and forty-seven millions of greenbacks and three hundred and sixteen millions of national-bank notes, amounting together to some six hundred and sixty millions of paper currency. That is now used for the purpose of the business transactions of the country. The point to which I wish to direct the attention of the committee and of the Secretary of the Treasury is, whether the three hundred millions of legal tenders are not absolutely requisite for the business purposes of the country, and whether, therefore, there will be any very great desire to exchange them for gold.

Secretary SHERMAN. I do not think we have a great excess of currency now. These bankers say that there is not enough of currency. So long as there is a want of confidence in our ability to resume, it is likely that the greenbacks will be presented for redemption to some extent; but if we were so strong that the public mind was satisfied of our ability to resume, there would be no motive to present notes for redemption (especially when they may be redeemed in silver). Then, I agree that these notes will not be presented.

Mr. FORT. Would not a premium of 1 per cent. run these notes in for redemption, even with confidence restored?

Secretary SHERMAN. O, yes; but we must abolish the 1 per cent. difference.

Mr. PHILLIPS. Can you state any distinction between legal-tender notes and national-bank notes in regard to the obligation of redemption?

Secretary SHERMAN. Certainly, sir. We have nothing to do with the redemption of the national-bank notes. The banks can take care of that themselves, and they are doing it now. They have an enormous reserve.

Mr. PHILLIPS. It is stated in the papers of Saturday that you ordered the retirement of $767,000 of legal tender notes for last month.

Secretary SHERMAN. Certainly. The law explicitly required that.

Mr. PHILLIPS. I thought that the law left it to your discretion.

Secretary SHERMAN. Not at all. The Treasurer of the United States, at the end of each month, on the report of the Comptroller of the Currency that such an amount of national-bank notes has been issued, retires and redeems from his currency reserves 80 per cent. of greenbacks. I have nothing to do with it.

Mr. FORT. Do you think that good policy?

Secretary SHERMAN. I do. That must be continued until the amount of greenbacks is reduced to $300,000,000.

Mr. PHILLIPS. Do you think it safe to reduce the volume of greenbacks to $300,000,000?

Secretary SHERMAN. I think $300,000,000 is enough.

Mr. PHILLIPS. Can you not safely resume unless you reduce the amount of greenbacks to $300,000,000?

Secretary SHERMAN. I cannot say that. The law provides a mode by which the currency can be reduced to $300,000,000.

Mr. HARDENBERGH. If Congress should adjourn, with the state of the finances as they are now, and without additional legislation, and with resumption fixed to take place on the 1st of January next, do you not suppose that the national banks will have to buy from thirty to fifty millions of gold to make themselves strong enough to meet resumption?

Secretary SHERMAN. Certainly; they are doing it largely now.

Mr. FORT. Do you still desire to cancel the forty-seven millions of legal tenders now outstanding in excess of the three hundred millions.

Secretary SHERMAN. I think it wise to stand by the present law.

The CHAIRMAN. Do you actually destroy this eighty per cent. of greenbacks?

Secretary SHERMAN. We reduce it monthly. The amount is stated in every debt-statement. It is an actual destruction of the greenbacks. The idea was that $300,000,000 of greenbacks can be easily and surely maintained at par in coin.

Mr. BELL. Is it your judgment that the volume of currency at $300,000,000 will be adequate to the business wants of the country?

Secretary SHERMAN. No; in my judgment the currency will be increased from time to time by the free action of the national banks, and I believe that the amount of circulation in this country, where we are accustomed to paper money, will be always largely in excess of what it would be in old countries where they hoard coin.

Mr. EWING. And in excess of what it is now?

Secretary SHERMAN. I am inclined to think that we can maintain the present volume of circulation—six hundred millions—but that is a larger paper circulation than was ever maintained by any other country. That is a question for the banks to decide for themselves.

Mr. PHILLIPS. Has not the volume of national-bank notes been steadily reduced since the passage of the resumption act?

Secretary SHERMAN. Certainly; because the banks chose to retire them. They have a right to do that, and they chose to retire them; I cannot control that. The Secretary of the Treasury has no more to do with the process of reducing the currency or of increasing it than any of you gentlemen—not near so much, because you can stop it and I cannot; I simply execute the law.

Mr. EWING. In your statement to the Senate Finance Committee I find the following:

TREASURY OF THE UNITED STATES,
Washington, March 18, 1878.

SIR: In accordance with your request, I have the honor to state the amount of gold and silver in the Treasury on the 23th ultimo, the date of the last debt-statement, which is as follows, viz:

Gold coin... $117,151,455 62
Gold bullion 7,937,300 21
                                                                        $125,088,755 98

Less amount to credit of disbursing-officers and outstanding checks.................................. 6,189,626 60
Gold-certificates actually outstanding 44,498,500 00
Called bonds and interest............................ 6,818,677 29
Interest due and unpaid.............................. 4,909,705 21
                                                                        62,416,509 10

Available gold coin and bullion...................... 62,672,246 88
Available silver coin, fractional.................... 5,972,895 42
Available silver bullion............................. 3,130,718 31

Total available gold and silver...................... 71,775,860 56

According to this statement, the amount of gold and silver coin and bullion applicable to resumption, belonging to the United States on the last day of February, 1878, was $71,775,000. You then say that you have practically, for business purposes, $20,000,000 more of coin applicable to resumption, because you have deducted from the gold in the Treasury four items, making an aggregate of about $62,000,000, part of which you assume that you can use.

Secretary SHERMAN. Yes, sir.

Mr. EWING. Now, I ask you which of those items so deducted are practically available for resumption ?

Secretary SHERMAN. The amount to the credit of disbursing-officers and outstanding checks varies but very little, because it rarely, if ever, gets below $5,000,000, and it varies from that up (the amount in process of disbursement), so that you can very fairly anticipate that fact (it is a business fact), just as a merchant can anticipate the coming in of his bills receivable.

Mr. EWING. Is not that banking ?

Secretary SHERMAN. Every man does banking in that sense.

Mr. EWING. Would the Treasury be justified in disregarding outstanding existing interest obligations by applying the coin which was set apart to meet those obligations to the redemption of legal-tender notes ?

Secretary SHERMAN. The Treasury will do just what any prudent individual will do; it will anticipate the demands upon it, and always have money to meet those demands. It is sufficient for me to say that the law authorizes the use in anticipation of coin-certificates. The amount of coin-certificates that may be issued can be 20 per cent. in excess of actual coin. The Secretary of the Treasury, from the known certainty that these coin-certificates will not be and cannot be presented all at once, and are not likely to be diminished in amount, can issue 20 per cent. in excess of the actual coin on deposit.

Mr. EWING. Yes, the law gives you that authority. What would 20 per cent. of the coin-certificates amount to ?

Secretary SHERMAN. Nearly $9,000,000.

Mr. EWING. So that you might at this time issue coin-certificates to the amount of $9,000,000 beyond the amount of coin now in the Treasury ?

Secretary SHERMAN. Yes, sir. The law authorizes that. I will say, however, that it has not been done. As to the next item, "Called bonds and interest"—$6,818,677—that amount is in the Treasury, and is always there. There is interest due and carried on the debt-statement for twenty or thirty years; but we count it as a demand that we must provide for, and it is covered by this deduction.

Mr. EWING. How much of that amount is for called bonds and interest on such bonds?

Secretary SHERMAN. The whole of it. We have now in the Treasury over $7,000,000 due to "called bonds and interest"—that is, bonds that are due and not bearing interest, but that are not presented for payment. Sometimes bonds come in three or four years after they are due, and they are then paid.

Mr. EWING. Can anything approaching that amount have gone beyond the ninety days when the payment of interest stops?

Secretary SHERMAN. Every dollar of that has gone beyond the ninety days. Whether that amount will be continuously in the Treasury is only to be told by a comparison of the statements of "called bonds and interest." I have no doubt that some of that amount will never be called for. You will find by reference to the monthly statements that the amount varies from month to month, but it is an item which can be counted on with almost as much certainty as any other item.

Mr. Ewing. I notice from the Treasury report that the whole "slack" from the beginning of the government to August, 1877, is less than $2,000,000 out of the $7,000,000 of aggregate of called bonds and interest unpaid to date. I don't think you can very safely assume that the $5,000,000 of bonds under recent calls will not be presented.

Secretary Sherman. On the contrary, under the last call—which is charged up and included in this last statement (a call of $10,000,000, made on the 6th of December last and maturing on the 6th of March)— but $7,000,000 of bonds had been presented on the day before yesterday, leaving $3,000,000 not presented. That leaves two or three millions of that particular call. I do not say that you can rely upon it with absolute certainty.

Mr. Ewing. This inquiry is to ascertain how much gold and silver can be certainly relied upon to redeem legal-tender notes.

Secretary Sherman. Well, I think you can fairly count on at least one-half of this $6,818,677 of " called bonds and interest." In all human probability there will be three or four millions of that amount that will not be called for.

Mr. Ewing. Within what time ?

Secretary Sherman. There will be that balance on that account all the time, because we are going on to make calls all the time.

Mr. Ewing. But if you are pushed to get coin enough to redeem legal-tender notes you are certainly not going to continue the call of bonds ; so that probably that item will disappear from your resources.

Secretary Sherman. In my judgment, we will go on and make those calls. Last year we accumulated $60,000,000 of actual gold in the Treasury, while at the same time we were making calls at the rate of $1,000,000 a day ; and therefore your conclusion does not follow. If we had this question of resumption fixed beyond doubt, and if the people understood that it was to come, the bonds would be taken promptly and the calls would be rapid ; because accumulation for resumption accompanies and is increased by refunding. The actual experiment shows it. Whenever we have made calls we have accumulated coin, until last December, when, by the agitation created here in Congress, it ceased. My calls were outstanding, but the bonds did not sell.

Mr. Ewing. We are trying to ascertain the amount of coin which you can certainly use in redeeming legal-tender notes; and you say that in an exigency you can use that item of $6,818,677 of " called bonds and interest," or a portion of it. It seems to me that if the exigency arises you will be in such a condition that you will not be calling bonds and increasing your coin demand ; and, therefore, that that fund is not available, and that you cannot safely draw upon it to redeem legal-tender notes ; or if you do so in an extremity, you may not only fail of resumption, but also fail of paying the interest and principal of the debt.

Secretary Sherman. I say that having $62,000,000 of coin in our possession subject to demand liabilities (an aggregate sum), which by the experience of nine years is rarely diminished to the amount of ten or fifteen per cent. (never falling below $50,000,000, and sometimes going up as high as $80,000,000), we can fairly count that, in any probable state of circumstances at least $18,000,000 of that amount will be in the Treasury—not to be used (because I do not anticipate that our reserve will ever be drawn down to that), but that we may fairly count upon it as in the Treasury.

Mr. Ewing. This accumulation has been during the period when legal-tender notes were not redeemable, but you certainly cannot assume that, because you have had that accumulation of coin in the Treasury heretofore when there was no redemption of legal-tender notes, you will continue to have it after redemption begins ?

Secretary SHERMAN. I think we can assume if, when gold was not in circulation, there was a gold balance in the Treasury subject to demand without much variation, that, when all transactions are based on coin or paper redeemable in coin, this coin will remain in the Treasury. I believe that one of the first effects of resumption will be to increase the deposit of coin in the Treasury, because paper will be so much more convenient in all the transactions of life that paper will be used and the coin will be deposited with us. The subtreasury in New York will be, like the Bank of England, the place of deposit for all the coin of the country; and coin certificates or greenbacks will be used for all current transactions, leaving the coin only to be drawn to meet the demands of foreign trade or the mutations and changes of supply and demand.

The CHAIRMAN. That would depend entirely upon the balance of trade ?

Secretary SHERMAN. Very much.

The CHAIRMAN. That would be the key of the situation ?

Secretary SHERMAN. Yes, sir.

Mr. EWING. You say, then, that at least $3,000,000 of this $6,818,677 for " called bonds and interest" might be used, if necessary, in the redemption of legal-tender notes ?

Secretary SHERMAN. Practically. I would say that at least one-third of the amount, $2,000,000, might be so used. The next item of $4,909,705, "interest due and unpaid," stands in about the same position ; in fact, it is more stable than the other.

Mr. EWING. You think that $2,000,000 of that could be used ?

Secretary SHERMAN. Yes, and perhaps more. Here (showing a debt statement) are the items of this "interest due and unpaid;" much of it is on old loans. Very often people do not collect their coupons, but leave the interest to accumulate, so that this interest item is even more stable than the other item. This is the " interest due and unpaid " on outstanding bonds; the other is "the interest and principal of called bonds."

Mr. EWING. I see that this "interest due and unpaid" is made up chiefly on bonds not yet due. It therefore cannot run along.

Secretary SHERMAN. That always follows. Suppose a man who owns $10,000 of bonds neglects to cut off the coupons when they are due and lets them run for two or three months without collecting the interest, he is likely to do the same thing the next time.

Mr. EWING. But suppose it were understood that the Treasury was short of gold, would it not be likely that these overdue coupons would be run in for collection ? In other words, could you safely use that fund to redeem legal-tender notes if you are pushed to that point ?

Secretary SHERMAN. I do not think I would have occasion to use that fund, but I simply say (as I have said to the Senate committee) that while we can only surely count upon the actual coin on hand over and above our coin liabilities, we can yet, as business men, fairly understand that all of these demands, of which I have given the items, will not be presented at the same time, and that there will always be a balance of at least eighteen millions of them.

Mr. EWING. Do you count any of the coin-certificates in that category ?

Secretary SHERMAN. Yes; I count 20 per cent. on coin-certificates.

Mr. EWING. You propose to issue 20 per cent. of new certificates beyond the amount of gold on hand ?

Secretary SHERMAN. Yes, we could.

Mr. EWING. Which you may use for the redemption of legal-tender notes?

Secretary SHERMAN. I do not think I ever would, except in case of necessity, but the law authorizes it.

Mr. PHILLIPS. Have not our revenues, both from internal revenue and imports, been decreasing of late?

Secretary SHERMAN. Yes, but we have more gold revenue than we have gold expenditures.

Mr. PHILLIPS. But have not the revenues been decreasing this year as compared with the past year?

Secretary SHERMAN. Very largely this winter—especially in the whisky tax.

Mr. PHILLIPS. And will not the recent law in regard to whisky still further decrease the revenue?

Secretary SHERMAN. That gets me into legislative grounds, and I think you had better settle that question among yourselves. There is no doubt but that we will have a surplus revenue to the extent of a portion of the sinking-fund. I do not think that a deficiency can equal the sinking-fund.

Mr. PHILLIPS. The sale of bonds has been stopped?

Secretary SHERMAN. Yes, but we can renew their sale if we pay a higher rate of interest—if we issue 4½ per cent. bonds. The time was (ever since I have been in public life) that it would have been looked upon as very remarkable to sell bonds at less than 4½ per cent., and we are getting very strong when we refuse to sell bonds at 4½ per cent. Never before in the history of the government have bonds been issued and sold at par at so low a rate of interest as four per cent.

Mr. PHILLIPS. You state that we have coin interest to pay to the amount of ninety millions a year. Do you think it would be safe to undertake resumption with that burden resting upon us?

Secretary SHERMAN. Clearly. If we have the power to reissue legal-tender notes at par, and the power to sell bonds, if necessary, we can undoubtedly keep the notes at par. Redemption would not go far before legal-tender notes would become scarce. I have stated that there were $70,000,000 of those legal-tender notes in our vaults, and there are also $70,000,000 of them in the custody of the national banks, whose interest it would be to keep them in their vaults.

Mr. PHILLIPS. Would it not be more to their interest to have the coin?

Secretary SHERMAN. These legal-tender notes are scattered all over the country.

Mr. PHILLIPS. The interest of the banks to get the gold might prompt them to send in these greenbacks for redemption.

Secretary SHERMAN. If you ask me whether 347 millions of legal-tender notes can be all paid with a hundred millions of coin if they are all presented on the same day, I will say no; but, with 600 millions of currency, you cannot purchase all the wheat and corn in the country in the same day.

Mr. PHILLIPS. Will not the mere act of resumption create a demand for gold which does not now exist?

Secretary SHERMAN. On the contrary, I think it will diminish the demand for gold. What would they want gold for?

Mr. PHILLIPS. These banks may wish to resume.

Secretary SHERMAN. They would rather resume in greenbacks. They deposit their gold with us for safe-keeping.

H. Mis. 48——2

Mr. FORT. Would there not be a temptation for the banks to exchange their greenbacks for gold ?

Secretary SHERMAN. I do not see what object they would have in doing it.

Mr. FORT. They would do it merely for the premium.

Secretary SHERMAN. But there would not be any premium.

Mr. EWING. How much of this item of "interest due and unpaid," $4,909,705, do you say may be counted as applicable to resumption ?

Secretary SHERMAN. I would say about one-third of it.

Mr. EWING. That will be one million three hundred thousand.

Secretary SHERMAN. I never went into the division of this thing.

Mr. EWING. Then the item of " amount to credit of disbursing officers and outstanding checks," $6,189,626. How much of that can be used for resumption ?

Secretary SHERMAN. You may count on the whole of it if you choose ; because it is really only money in the course of disbursement. We always have in the hands of disbursing officers large sums of money, and every disbursing officer has a balance on hand, and we can reduce those balances to a large extent, or cut them off entirely.

Mr. EWING. You include "outstanding checks"; do you think you could count the whole sum they represent as part of the funds that could be used ?

Secretary SHERMAN. No, sir.

Mr. EWING. How much of it ?

Secretary SHERMAN. I cannot tell ; because I cannot tell how much of this item is for " outstanding checks" and how much to the credit of disbursing officers.

Mr. EWING. Exclusive of those items you would only have on your theory $12,300,000 which you could add to the $62,000,000.

Secretary SHERMAN. It is totally immaterial whether you count that in or count it out. As I said before, my reliance would be on the actual coin reserve—to be increased as I have stated. I do not propose to resume on seventy-one millions of coin.

Mr. EWING. It strikes me that the addition of seventeen or eighteen millions, drawn from these four items, is not safe in calculating the resources for resumption.

Secretary SHERMAN. I think that if you ask any banker in New York how much of that fund is available for resumption purposes, he will put it higher than I do.

Mr. EWING. As a banker?

Secretary SHERMAN. As long as we are issuing United States notes, redeemable on demand, we are in the banking business.

Mr. EWING. And take the bankers' chances ?

Secretary SHERMAN. We do it as a matter of course. We save the interest and have to do as bankers do.

Mr. EWING. You have got here under the item of " called bonds and interest " only $6,818,677. Has there not been a call of $10,000,000 since ?

Secretary SHERMAN. No ; there has been no call since. The last statement which you get to-day will include these " called bonds." The last call was made on the 6th of December, 1877, and matured on the 6th of March, 1878. .It has been covered—about half of the amount—by the sale of bonds since the call issued.

Mr. EWING. Does this statement include all of the called bonds unpaid on the first of February, 1878 ?

Secretary SHERMAN. Yes, sir; all the called bonds that matured at that date.

Mr. FORT. What is the cost of selling bonds, including the expenses of the syndicate?

Secretary SHERMAN. One half of one per cent. is the limit under the law and our contract with the syndicate. The syndicate pays all the cost, including engraving, &c., out of the half of one per cent. Under the popular loan we pay one-fourth of one per cent. commission and pay the expenses out of the other fourth.

Mr. EWING. Going back to your statement before the Finance Committee, you add to the sixty-two millions of gold five millions nine hundred and seventy-two thousand dollars of fractional silver coin; do you regard that as available for resumption?

Secretary SHERMAN. Undoubtedly. We can issue that silver coin in exchange for United States notes to the full extent of the outstanding fractional currency; but, in my judgment, Congress ought to pass a law enlarging the limit of subsidiary silver to fifty million dollars.

Mr. EWING. Such an exchange would be a voluntary exchange on the part of the holder of legal-tender notes. I am not speaking of what you can buy with the subsidiary silver coin, but as to whether it is available for the *redemption* of legal-tender notes when presented.

Secretary SHERMAN. Yes; in my judgment that five millions of dollars will be all absorbed before the first of January.

Mr. EWING. But we are speaking of this as a redemption fund for the legal-tender notes after the first of January.

Secretary SHERMAN. If the five millions of subsidiary silver coin be paid out in exchange for United States notes or in current expenses, there will be left in the Treasury just so much the more current revenue which will be in gold.

Mr. EWING. But after resumption day you do not regard fractional silver as available for the purposes of redemption?

Secretary SHERMAN. Only to a small amount. We will still exchange silver coin for United States notes. But I think the whole amount now on hand will be paid out and gold will take its place.

Mr. EWING. The resumption law provides that the redemption of legal-tender notes shall be in sums of $50 and upward, and fractional silver currency is not a legal tender above $5. How, then, can it be counted upon as part of the *redemption* fund?

Secretary SHERMAN. Simply because it can be, and will be, probably, exchanged, as needed, for United States notes.

Mr. EWING. But after the first of January can it be used as part of the redemption fund?

Secretary SHERMAN. Yes, I think so; if it is used for the redemption of United States notes.

Mr. EWING. It is not a legal-tender?

Secretary SHERMAN. That makes no difference. People come to us every day with United States notes for silver currency.

Mr. EWING. But I am speaking of using this fractional silver currency for the redemption contemplated by the law.

Secretary SHERMAN. I regard redemption as simply meaning paying, according to law, the United States notes in the coin which the holder has a right to demand. Any holder of a United States note may now come to the Treasury and ask to be paid in subsidiary silver coin. After the first of January we will pay him in silver dollars or in gold coin, just as he prefers. If we should redeem United States notes between now and the first of January to the extent of five millions of dollars, we have in place of it the revenue which comes into Treasury—probably in gold.

Mr. EWING. My point is this: that fractional silver coin cannot be counted as a fund with which to redeem, after the first of January, United States notes, because it is not a legal tender for as much as $50, and because, under the law, the presentation of legal-tender notes must be in sums of $50 and upward.

Secretary SHERMAN. I do not think it material for us to discuss that question, because that five millions of subsidiary silver coin will be used in exchange for United States notes precisely as the silver dollars will be.

The CHAIRMAN. You regard it as an asset in the Treasury for all the purposes of the resumption bill?

Secretary SHERMAN. Certainly. If you really want to drive me into the position, I can simply say that we can convert subsidiary silver coin into silver dollars and then we can pay it out. It is money there in the Treasury available for the payment of United States notes.

Mr. EWING. Might you not as well put in United States notes as money available for redemption?

Secretary SHERMAN. No; I think not. This subsidiary currency would, in the ordinary course of business, be paid out in lieu of other revenue, and would be replaced by gold or silver.

Mr. EWING. In the statement made on the 26th of February to this committee by the Treasurer, he says: "I am informed by the Director of the Mint that the amount of unpaid deposits belonging to private individuals and held by the mints and assay-offices on January 1, 1878, amounted to $2,114,000." Is that a proper deduction from the coin on hand?

Secretary SHERMAN. No, sir; that is a mint account.

Mr. EWING. But the amount in the mints is credited in your table.

Secretary SHERMAN. Only the amount belonging to the United States. There are private deposits of bullion under the law. That is a private deposit for trade-dollars. It is not a liability.

Mr. EWING. That is, the gold and silver are not counted in the statement of the amount in the mints?

Secretary SHERMAN. No, sir; that debit is for gold and silver deposited by private individuals for their own use.

Mr. EWING. In this statement you have got the available sum on hand at $71,000,000, without any deduction for accruing interest?

Secretary SHERMAN. Yes, sir.

Mr. EWING. Now, the interest which is accruing on bonds is to be paid by gold which has been accruing from customs, *pari passu?*

Secretary SHERMAN. Yes, sir.

Mr. EWING. You count all the gold thus coming in from customs as applicable to resumption, and yet here is a charge upon it of $17,277,000, up to the last of February, for accruing interest?

Secretary SHERMAN. The answer to that is that the interest is not due. If the interest is accruing, we have also revenue accruing. We have goods deposited with us and bonds issued for customs duties, but we do not count this as revenue, although the revenue is accruing with absolute certainty of payment, and will be paid within a year.

Mr. EWING. It is not fixed in amount?

Secretary SHERMAN. O, yes. The entries are liquidated and ascertained, and we hold the goods in bond ; but we do not call that revenue, because it is not paid ; and so it is with accruing interest. Interest, as it accrues, we count as such, but interest accruing will be met before it becomes due by revenue accruing.

Mr. EWING. But you have already credited your whole accruing revenue to your resumption fund?

Secretary SHERMAN. No; we have credited our accrued revenue. We do not in either case credit the accruing or prospective revenue or the accruing or prospective interest.

Mr. EWING. That is *retrospective* interest. It has accumulated to the extent of over seventeen millions to the date of your statement.

Secretary SHERMAN. It is no more fixed than the revenue which is accruing. This question of whether, in our liabilities, interest not yet due shall be counted has been variously discussed, and many take a different view of it; but I take it that the point is this: Can that interest be demanded on the 1st of March or on the 1st of April? Certainly not. There is accruing interest from the 1st of January to the 1st of July; but it is not due until the 1st of July, and cannot be counted, therefore, as a demand liability until the 1st of July; and in the mean time our ample coin revenues come in, and a great deal more than cover the accruing interest.

Mr. EWING. But as a matter of fact, if you take out that seventeen millions of accruing interest and say that you put that apart as a resumption fund, you will be short of revenue to pay your interest and to create the sinking fund, as the law requires.

Secretary SHERMAN. If we are bound not only to get gold enough to pay what is due, but bound to get gold enough also to pay what may be due in six months, as a matter of course we can never resume.

Mr. EWING. I think it fair enough to say that whatever you have on hand now which has no ascertainable charge against it may be counted as a redemption fund for the greenbacks, trusting to future revenue to meet the future accruing interest and liabilities. But the difficulty about this statement is, that you have taken all the gold in hand now, and have not counted the accruing interest, which amounts to the very large sum of $17,227,000 up to the date of your statement, while the law expressly sets apart the gold that has been accruing from the customs to meet the interest which has been accruing during the same time.

Secretary SHERMAN. No; but to meet the interest which has accrued.

Mr. EWING. The statement, I think, makes an incorrect impression on the public mind as to the amount of gold actually on hand for resumption purposes.

Secretary SHERMAN. But, according to your idea, you would have us accumulate seventeen millions of gold more to-day to meet an obligation that is not to fall due until July.

Mr. EWING. No; but my idea is that in your statement you should have deducted the $17,227,000 of interest accruing up to date from the amount of gold on hand, because that gold is pledged and set apart by the law as a special fund to pay this interest, and is not applicable to resumption.

Secretary SHERMAN. But we have other gold as sure to come in as the 1st of July will come, to meet that interest.

Mr. EWING. Yes; and you have other obligations to meet to the amount of all the gold hereafter coming in.

Secretary SHERMAN. We cannot be expected to pay a debt before it is due.

Mr. EWING. The receipts from customs for the fiscal year 1877 were $130,956,000. The receipts this year will be less, as the imports have fallen off. The interest on the public debt last year was $97,124,000. That interest this year will be a little less. The sinking-fund this year, according to the statement of the Treasurer, is $35,424,000, and the law sets apart customs as expressly to the sinking-fund as it does to the interest on the public debt. Section 3694 of the Revised Statutes provides that "the coin paid for duties on imported goods shall be set apart as a special fund, and shall be applied as follows: 1st. To the payment in coin of the interest on the bonds and notes of the United States. 2d. To the purchase or payment of one per centum of the entire debt of the United States, to be made within each fiscal year, which is to be set apart as a sinking-fund, and the interest of which shall be in like manner applied to the purchase or payment of the public debt. 3d. The residue to be paid into the Treasury."

Now, here is a special appropriation by law of the receipts from customs to the extent of the sinking-fund and of the interest on the debt, and these two items will this year, evidently, amount to the whole receipts from customs.

Secretary SHERMAN. I have already explained the operation of the sinking-fund. If we should undertake to do what you say we ought to do—set aside that $35,000,000 and apply it for sinking-fund purposes—as a matter of course, there would be at once a deficiency in the payment of your own salaries, and of all the other expenses of the government. Now, this sinking-fund is a well-known technical fund, and has been known from the foundation of the government. It is really nothing but a pledge by Congress that it will provide revenues enough, not only to pay the expenses of the government, but to pay, in addition, the sinking-fund of one per cent. upon the debt. Therefore the sinking-fund has been always used simply as a representative of the balance of revenues over expenditures. The current expenditures are always taken from the amount of revenues, and the balance is applied to the sinking-fund. If there is a deficiency in the revenue, so that there is no balance to be applied to the sinking-fund, of course that is the fault of Congress in failing to provide revenues sufficient to cover the appropriations, and the amount to be applied to the sinking-fund. That has been the established custom of this and other countries.

Mr. EWING. I am not speaking about the custom, but the law. The law says that the coin paid for duties shall be set apart as a special fund, first, for the payment of coin-interest on the public debt; and, second, for the purchase of one per cent. of the debt each year, and for payment of interest upon the accumulated sinking-fund. Now, I do not see how any custom or usage of the department, or usage of other countries, can change the obligation of the statute.

Secretary SHERMAN. Let me look at the resumption act, if you have it there, and I will show you that not only does it do that in express terms, but it has been held to do it by every administration. (Referring to the law.) This clause has always been held to apply to the sinking-fund in the form of surplus revenue : "And to enable the Secretary of the Treasury to prepare and provide for the redemption by this act authorized and required, he is authorized to use any surplus revenue from time to time in the Treasury not otherwise appropriated, and to sell, issue, and dispose of, at not less than par in coin, either of the description of bonds, &c." This passed January 14, 1875. It has been held, under this appropriation made in 1875, of the surplus revenue, that the excess of revenue over expenditures could be applied under it without regard to the sinking-fund ; and that has been the construction put upon these words.

Mr. EWING. That is, by yourself, and Mr. Morrill, and Mr. Bristow, the only three Secretaries of the Treasury who administered that law.

Secretary SHERMAN. Yes, sir. That appropriation of surplus revenue has been held *pro tanto* to be an amendment of the act of 1870.

Mr. EWING. The words are " any surplus revenue from time to time in the Treasury not otherwise appropriated." Now in addition to section 3694 of the Revised Statutes which I have cited, there are, in sections 3688 and 3689, under the head of permanent annual appropriations, appropriations of the sums required for the sinking-fund. These provisions of law setting apart the customs as a special fund and permanently appropriating them to the sinking-fund, certainly are not affected by this provision of the resumption law, appropriating " any money in the Treasury not otherwise appropriated." ·

Secretary SHERMAN. I think it is; the words "surplus revenue" are not in it. That has been always construed to mean that sum of money which has been left after paying current expenses.

Mr. EWING. You mean always since the passage of the resumption law?

Secretary SHERMAN. I never saw that questioned. At all events it was so held, and acted upon when Mr. Bristow failed to make good the $16,305,421 of the sinking fund.

Mr. EWING. It was so held by the Secretary?

Secretary SHERMAN. Yes, sir; and was never questioned by Congress.

Mr. EWING. The subject may not have been looked into.

Secretary SHERMAN. That may be. As a matter of course, if Congress was to say that we should invest the sinking fund prior to and as against all appropriations made by Congress, it would leave a deficiency at once.

Mr. EWING. Congress has said it.

Secretary SHERMAN. I do not think that the fair construction. Still, that is a question for Congress and not for the Secretary. ·

Mr. EWING. The section from the Revised Statutes, which I have read, sets apart the duties on imported goods as a special fund for those two objects. A certain and permanent appropriation of the customs as a special fund, cannot reasonably be held to have been repealed or modified by this clause, which is usual to all laws—"out of any money in the Treasury not otherwise appropriated"—that is a common phrase in all statutes making appropriations.

Secretary SHERMAN. Look at the practical question. Would you have had Secretary Bristow, who met this difficulty in the first instance, refuse to pay the ordinary drafts for the expenses of the government to the extent of $16,000,000 ?

Mr. EWING. I would have had him execute the law, and most certainly and most especially I would not consent to the proposition that the resumption act overrides all the laws that preceded it, nor that the importance of resumption is so exigent and overwhelming, as that the permanent appropriations may be disregarded by the Executive in order to carry it into effect.

Secretary SHERMAN. All this you speak of occurred before the resumption law was passed. This very question about the application of the sinking-fund occurred June 30, 1874, and the resumption act was passed in 1875.

Mr. EWING. You are speaking of Mr. Bristow's interpretation ?

Secretary SHERMAN. And Mr. Morrill's.

Mr. EWING. Not Mr. Morrill's. The resumption law passed before Mr. Morrill became Secretary.

Secretary SHERMAN. Yes; but, at all events, that question was determined by the department and was acquiesced in certainly by Congress, and rightly acquiesced in. I certainly take my share of the fault, if there is anything wrong in it, for I was then in Congress, of acquiescing in the construction that the ordinary expenses of the government must be paid before the sinking fund is attended to, and that if there is any deficiency it must fall on the sinking-fund.

Mr. EWING. But what warrant can there be for a ruling that this general power to provide for resumption by using "any money in the Treasury not otherwise appropriated" shall override the permanent appropriation of receipts from customs as a special fund to pay interest on the public debt and to keep up the sinking-fund.

Secretary SHERMAN. The answer to that is, that the resumption act expressly authorizes the use of the surplus revenue and the proceeds of bonds to carry the resumption act into effect; and you will see that the resumption act has been carried into effect thus far by the sale of bonds, even in the purchase of the silver bullion in the first instance. Mr. Bristow sold $15,000,000 of five per cent. bonds and used the proceeds of those bonds in the purchase of silver bullion, and so all that I did under the resumption act was done by the sale of bonds.

Mr. EWING. There has been this year applied to the sinking fund $3,000,000 of fractional currency?

Secretary SHERMAN. Yes; and I do not know how many United States notes. We have redeemed largely United States notes. Last month we redeemed $700,000. All that goes into the sinking fund.

Mr. EWING. Why?

Secretary SHERMAN. Because it is a part of the debt which is redeemed under the operation of law.

Mr. EWING. The sinking-fund section (3694), which I have cited, contemplates the purchase of bonds.

Secretary SHERMAN. Not necessarily.

Mr. EWING. I think it does.

Secretary SHERMAN. United States notes are a portion of the public debt.

Mr. EWING. I think that the sinking fund act clearly contemplates the purchase of bonds only. The expression "one per cent. of the entire debt," simply means the mode of ascertaining the amount to be purchased. It further provides, "and interest on the debt so purchased."

Secretary SHERMAN. That is the computation of interest on the amount of debt as paid.

Mr. EWING. How do you compute interest on legal-tender notes?

Secretary SHERMAN. Probably at the current rate at which bonds are sold. I would not be able to tell you the exact rate last year, but the rule, I think, has been to compute the interest at the rate at which bonds were sold. Here is the computation. [Referring to it.] Page 18, Finance Report. I see that it is computed at 6 per cent.

Mr. EWING. Was there no redemption of bonds in 1876 for the sinking fund?

Secretary SHERMAN. Yes, a small amount.

Mr. EWING. This resumption law does not expressly provide that the legal-tender notes redeemed under it (80 per cent. of the issue of bank notes) shall be destroyed. They may be hereafter authorized to be reissued.

Secretary SHERMAN. These words in the act "until the amount outstanding shall be $300,000,000 of such legal-tender notes and no more," were held to mean a permanent retirement of notes in excess of that amount. If I ever had any doubt about that it was removed by the passage of the Revised Statutes, which re-enacts the old law about the reissue of United States notes. From that, taken with the resumption act, it seems plain that after the reduction of greenbacks to $300,000,000 had been reached, they may be reissued. The act provides that the reduction shall go on until the amount is reduced to $300,000,000 and no more.

Mr. EWING. I find according to the finance report of 1877, a deficiency in the sinking fund for that year of $9,225,000.

Secretary SHERMAN. That is correct.

Mr. EWING. And for 1876 a deficiency of $1,143,000; for 1875 a deficiency of $5,596,000; and for 1874 a deficiency of $16,305,000, making the total deficiency $32,670,000.

Secretary SHERMAN. I suppose that is correct.

Mr. EWING. If the gold received from the revenue had been applied, as this permanent appropriation requires, your stock of gold would be pretty largely reduced.

Secretary SHERMAN. Yes, and if the amount of money which had been applied to the sinking fund before the panic of 1873, in excess of the amount required by law, had been set apart for a resumption fund, we would have been at specie payments long ago, and that is what ought to have been done, in my judgment; but there is no use in " crying over spilled milk."

Mr. EWING. I understand that you feel at liberty under the usage to neglect any application to the sinking fund at all, if the purposes of the resumption law require it.

Secretary SHERMAN. No; I feel bound to do this, to apply the actual surplus revenue to the sinking fund; and that has been done. But when there is not sufficient surplus revenue to pay the sinking-fund I would let the deficit fall on the sinking fund. That is the way we have done.

Mr. EWING. And it has made a deficit in four years of $32,000,000.

Secretary SHERMAN. That is, the Government of the United States has failed to keep up the sinking-fund to that amount for the last four years.

Mr. EWING. And you do not feel required to apply any gold received from customs to the purchase of bonds for the sinking-fund?

Secretary SHERMAN. Except to the extent of the surplus revenue.

Mr. EWING. Even then you feel justified in paying the sinking fund in legal-tenders instead of in bonds.

Secretary SHERMAN. Yes; that is the construction put upon the law. We have a right to count the legal tenders and fractional currency returned under the operations of the law as so much debt paid. We do not retire any legal-tenders under any circumstances except in consequence of the issue of the national-bank notes; but when legal-tender notes are retired in that way, we count them as so much debt paid and we credit them to the sinking fund.

Mr. EWING. And your construction of the statute is that the debt canceled must not necessarily be a bonded debt.

Secretary SHERMAN. That is the construction.

Mr. EWING. But that it may be a debt bearing no interest?

Secretary SHERMAN. Yes, sir.

Mr. EWING. And the Secretary of the Treasury is at liberty to fix the rate of interest on it?

Secretary SHERMAN. No; I do not wish to answer that in the affirmative, because my impression was that the interest was counted at the current rate. I have never had occasion yet to fix the interest.

Mr. Ewing. In your statement to the Finance Committee of the Senate, as to the preparation the national banks have made for resumption, you have given the banks' statement showing the amount of gold held by them on December 28, 1877, as $5,506,556.

Secretary Sherman. That is the amount held by the New York City banks alone.

Mr. Ewing. No; that is the amount held by all the national banks. All the national banks of the United States held $5,506,000 of gold coin on the 28th of December last.

Secretary Sherman. The banks have gold certificates, however. They own that gold in the Treasury and we do not count it as ours at all.

Mr. Ewing. Is it counted in the $125,000,000 ?

Secretary Sherman. Yes. The amount of the specie of the banks, including gold-certificates, was, on the 28th of December, 1877, $32,907,750. That was the amount of coin and gold-certificates held by the national banks; but that amount is largely increased now. (See Appendix No. 6.)

Mr. Ewing. Outside of the Treasury there is, it appears, $5,506,556 of gold in the banks. Do you think the actual gold coin in the banks has largely increased since then ?

Secretary Sherman. I do not know about that ; I think it has. There is an increase in the commercial cities; but I do not like to speak positively upon that point, because in a day or two you will have the actual returns from all those banks.

Mr. Ewing. Adding the certificates held by the banks, $23,000,000, to the $5,000,000 of gold coin, you get the extent of their preparation for resumption.

Secretary Sherman. Yes, sir.

Mr. Ewing. Unless you count the fractional silver coin as a redemption fund, which it seems to me it is not.

Secretary Sherman. The amount of gold held by the New York banks alone, including gold certificates, is $5,000,000 more to-day than the whole gold and silver coin in all the banks of the United States in December last.

Mr. Ewing. Including gold-certificates ?

Secretary Sherman. Yes, including certificates. The amount is $37,432,000, or $5,000,000 more than the whole amount in all the banks in the United States in December last. Now, as to how much gold has increased in the other banks I cannot say, but we will have the returns in a day or two, and perhaps in time to attach to this statement.

Mr. Ewing. Probably $40,000,000 of gold coin and certificates together will represent the preparation of the national banks for resumption.

Secretary Sherman. It is more than that. The increase in the New York national banks alone from December to March was $13,000,000. All the great body of these coin-certificates is held by banks and bankers.

Mr. Ewing. Do you think the aggregate of gold coin and certificates in the hands of the national banks would run up to $45,000,000 ?

Secretary Sherman. I should think so.

Mr. Ewing. That $45,000,000, assumed to be held by the national banks and whatever amount you have in the Treasury belonging to the United States applicable to resumption, represents the whole preparation for the redemption of the $647,000,000 of paper money ?

Secretary SHERMAN. So far as the national banks are concerned they have enormous resources. They are only bound to redeem their notes in United States notes, of which they have $70,000,000 on hand; they have also cash resources of various kinds as shown by this table, and very large ones. They have surplus profits to the amount of $173,000,000 over and above their capital stock. They have resources which will enable them to redeem in United States notes with great facility.

Mr. EWING. Their surplus profits are invested largely in buildings.

Secretary SHERMAN. They have invested largely in United States bonds. They have United States bonds on hand to the amount of nearly four hundred millions of dollars. They have $343,000,000 to secure their currency. Then they have bonds to secure deposits; and they have other United States bonds on hand; and they have very large cash funds. As a matter of course they have also very large loans and discounts, and they are liable to their depositors to a very large sum. But they have ample cash resources.

Mr. EWING. But I am speaking of the amount of gold and silver they have for resumption.

Secretary SHERMAN. The banks do not have to redeem any notes in gold; they redeem in United States notes.

Mr. EWING. After all, the problem is to float $647,000,000 of paper money redeemable in coin.

Secretary SHERMAN. Yes.

Mr. EWING. Now, is not the drain upon the government practically the same to the extent of the aggregate of the greenback circulation ($348,000,000), as though the entire circulation were money?

Secretary SHERMAN. I say no, emphatically; and all experience in other systems of banks would also say no. The truth is, the Government of the United States has nothing to do with the banks any more than it has to do with the other corporations and merchants of the country. The banks are as separate and distinct corporations as they can possibly be made. The United States have got to redeem $348,000,000 of legal tender notes, or to make them at par with coin. You recollect what I said before, that we have seventy millions undisputed money in coin.

Mr. EWING. I beg leave to say that I regard the statement as incorrect.

Secretary SHERMAN. Let me go on. We have seventy millions of coin and then we have seventy millions of currency in our possession, some of which at least belongs to us, and none of which is likely to be called for, unless it may be a portion of the certificates of deposit, amounting together to $26,000,000. Then we have these obligations on the part of the banks, which are not fictitious persons but strong corporations. They hold at least seventy millions in our notes and forty millions of gold or gold certificates in their vaults as a reserve at all times. Their notes are absolutely secured by United States bonds, so that if you take that into consideration it is very easy for us to resume. And then you must remember that the body of our notes is in circulation all over this broad country, scattered everywhere from one end of the land to the other. Now, is it likely that these notes are going to be rushed in for payment of them in coin?

Mr. EWING. I think it is.

Secretary SHERMAN. I say no; you have no confidence.

Mr. EWING. I have met very few who have confidence.

Secretary SHERMAN. I say that if you strengthen this reserve from seventy millions to from one hundred and twenty millions to one hundred and fifty millions, with power in the Secretary of the Treasury to sell bonds if necessary, and with power to reissue greenbacks, there is no danger of breaking the government. I do not think that anybody desires that. Everybody will be glad that the contest is over. Let us look out for ourselves and let the banks look out for themselves. The banks are not interested in running in our notes to get coin for them to embarrass us. On the contrary, these legal-tender notes are their money, and as long as they have them, they cannot be broken. Their notes are payable in our notes, and if they keep a strong reserve of our notes (and they will be interested in keeping a strong reserve), they give us aid practically by giving employment to our notes. There is no motive for them (unless there be a fear that we are not able to pay) to rush in and demand payment of our notes in coin. Now I can see very well that if we had a reserve of $130,000,000 of coin, with no demand liabilities whatever except for those legal-tender notes, we can maintain those notes at par in coin—scattered as they are over this country. It seems to me that there is no difficulty about it.

Mr. EWING. My question was this: Whether the general government, to the extent of its whole paper circulation outstanding, must not respond to the demands of the holders of the $647,000,000 of paper currency for conversion into coin?

Secretary SHERMAN. The government is bound to respond, to the extent of the amount of United States notes outstanding, but not one step farther.

Mr. EWING. Of course not.

Secretary SHERMAN. Very well. That is only $300,000,000. It is just as if Great Britain was behind that $300,000,000 of bank-notes—a separate and distinct power. We are under no obligation to redeem the national bank notes. On the contrary the banks are under obligation to redeem their own notes in our notes and we hold ample security for that. Anybody can present a national bank note at the Treasury, and the Treasury is ready to redeem it, having a deposit of 5 per cent. which the banks must keep good to redeem national bank notes. The banks are obliged to redeem their own notes in our notes, and they are therefore desirous to get our notes.

Mr. EWING. Suppose that through lack of confidence in your ability to maintain resumption, with the small accumulation of gold that you can obtain, there should be a demand for fifty millions of coin in any one month in New York. It makes no difference whether the demand is made on the banks for legal tenders, and then the legal tenders be sent to the Treasury for redemption, or whether the demand is directly on the Treasury, you have got to respond to the whole of that demand, and the gold has got to come out of the Treasury, because the banks have practically none in their vaults.

Secretary SHERMAN. It is scarcely a supposable proposition that you put to me that they could gather together in one mass an amount of legal-tender notes to break the Treasury if this reserve is anything like what I say. You can see as a matter of course that there are times when the Bank of England could not meet a demand for 25,000,000 pounds sterling in gold for bank notes. Perhaps at times the demand for half that amount would break it. But actual experiment shows that such a thing is practically impossible. The idea of accumulating $75,000,000 or $100,000,000 of United States notes and carrying them to the Treasury in the course of a month is practically impossible. The commencement of such a scheme as that would make legal-tender notes so scarce that it would be impossible to get them, and the very scarcity would increase their value so that they would be equal to coin.

Mr. EWING. They could very readily present at least their coin-certificates for redemption.

Secretary SHERMAN. Where are they? Scattered all over the country. The whole amount of money, including currency certificates in the city of New York, which is the great commercial deposit of the country, is only twenty million dollars, and they never get more than that. That is the amount of the aggregate. If they gathered every note and every certificate in all the national banks of New York, they would amount to twenty millions of dollars; and is it to be supposed that they would do that? Unless you maintain that we require to have as much gold on hand as there is paper money outstanding before we can have resumption, I do not see any difficulty about it.

Mr. EWING. Did I understand you to say that a demand for half of twenty five million pounds sterling on the Bank of England would break the bank?

Secretary SHERMAN. I do not know how much the reserve of the Bank of England is now, but the Bank of England, like all banks owe vast amounts of demand liabilities besides their notes. It holds the deposits of England. Every banking house in England almost, has an account in the Bank of England; and, therefore the danger which threatens the Bank of England would be the calling in of the deposits, and if notes to the amount of ten million pounds sterling were presented, in addition to the call of depositors, there would be such a draft upon the resources of the bank that the bank would have to suspend. But the advantage of our government now is that we have no demand liabilities not covered by actual money on hand. These national banks have six hundred million dollars due to depositors on call, but they have facilities to meet that liability. The strength of the United States Government is so much the greater from the fact that it owes nothing but these notes.

Mr. EWING. The gold coin and bullion of the Bank of England was, in December, 1877, one hundred and twenty-seven million dollars, and its entire circulation one hundred and thirty-three millions, so that it could pay its notes almost dollar for dollar.

Secretary SHERMAN. Yes; but add one hundred and twenty millions more that the bank is liable to be drawn upon for its deposits. How much does the bank owe its depositors?

Mr. EWING. One hundred and thirty-one million dollars.

Secretary SHERMAN. There is the danger. The call on the deposits might break it down.

Mr. EWING. Yet you do not seem afraid of the call of over six hundred millions of deposits of the national banks.

Secretary SHERMAN. I say that the national banks have ample resources in currency and United States bonds.

Mr. EWING. To pay the six hundred millions of deposits and to keep afloat three hundred and twenty millions of currency?

Secretary SHERMAN. They can not do it in a day, because it is not possible for the depositors to draw out their deposits in a day.

Mr. EWING. But contrast their situation with the situation of the Bank of England. The Bank of England has in circulation and deposits combined two hundred and sixty-six millions of dollars, and it has one hundred and twenty millions of coin against its circulation and deposits. Our national banks would have nine hundred and twenty millions of deposits and circulation, and have probably forty-five millions of coin to meet that; and yet you think that our national banks are in first-rate condition as compared with the Bank of England.

Secretary SHERMAN. You do not draw the distinction between our national banks and the Bank of England. The Bank of England occupies somewhat the position of our national government. But compare our situation with the Bank of England, and we are better off to-day.

Mr. EWING. You mean the Government of the United States?

Secretary SHERMAN. Yes. Let me give you the reason why. We have on hand one hundred and thirty-four millions of gold and silver; we have got seventy millions of paper money; which makes two hundred and four millions cash on hand in our Treasury.

Mr. EWING. You include money belonging to other people?

Secretary SHERMAN. So do you in your statement of the Bank of England.

Mr. EWING. This gold belongs to the bank.

Secretary SHERMAN. Take the full amount of the demand liabilities upon us and add them together, and then take the money which we have on hand, and we are in as good a condition as the Bank of England.

Mr. EWING. You are counting in the Treasury gold and legal-tenders which do not belong to the Treasury.

Secretary SHERMAN. No, that is a mistake.

Mr. EWING. The law expressly sets apart the gold on which certificates are issued as a special fund to redeem the certificates, so that it is not applicable to the redemption of legal-tender notes.

Secretary SHERMAN. But take the demand liabilities upon the United States and add them all together and then take all the money that we have got in the Treasury, and, I repeat, we are in a better condition than the Bank of England is.

Mr. BELL. Then your idea is that the question of sustaining resumption would depend, to a greater or less extent, on the amount of preparation on the day of resumption?

Secretary SHERMAN. Yes, sir; and after. I think we ought to be so strong that we can meet any reasonable demand made upon us.

Mr. EWING. The Bank of England has on hand in gold coin and bullion $120,000,000, and in the banking department $59,000,000 of notes.

Secretary SHERMAN. According to that the Bank of England has got $175,000,000 with which to pay $266,000,000. The total amount of demand liabilities on us is $407,000,000, and the total amount of coin and currency on hand $208,000,000. Add to that such an additional reserve as I propose to accumulate of $50,000,000, and it would make it $258,000,000 to meet $407,000,000, which is just about the proportion, according to the figures you give me, of $179,000,000, held by the Bank of England to meet its liabilities of $266,000,000. The disparity is not so great.

Mr. EWING. That is a statement of very little value, because you include gold and currency, which do not belong to us, and you lump it all in together; but if you put down your state of coin preparation for the obligations, which would be a coin demand after the 1st of January, 1879, you do not stand as favorably as the Bank of England.

Secretary SHERMAN. Considering that we have no demand liabilities except legal-tender notes, which have a pretty general circulation, I think that our condition on these figures is better than that of the Bank of England. Its liabilities are demand liabilities.

Mr. EWING. Will the reissue of legal-tender notes help you to maintain resumption?

Secretary SHERMAN. Yes; to have the power to reissue them; for if the greenbacks can be retained at par, and we can reissue them, it will save us from issuing bonds. We would only reissue greenbacks in exchange for coin or its equivalent. We would reissue them in payment of coin interest, but, as a matter of course, we could not reissue them unless they were equal to coin, just as the Bank of England would not issue a single note unless it was worth gold. We go on the supposition that the legal-tenders are on par with gold.

Mr. EWING. You have just now indicated a possibility of their not being at par with gold.

Secretary SHERMAN. No, sir.

Mr. EWING. You threw in the " if."

Secretary SHERMAN. The very moment you diminish the supply of greenbacks you bring them up to par again.

Mr. EWING. And your idea of reissuing greenbacks would be only to reissue them in exchange for coin?

Secretary SHERMAN. Or as a substitute for coin—to reissue them when they are at par with coin.

Mr. EWING. And you would reissue them for the purpose of increasing your coin supply?

Secretary SHERMAN. Yes, sir; practically. The public would be very willing to take the greenbacks if they were at par with coin, and as a matter of course they would be substitutes for coin.

The CHAIRMAN. Do you not think we could make them so if they were made receivable for four per cent. bonds?

Secretary SHERMAN. That is to be tried. I want to sell four per cent. bonds if I can. Whether, on actual experiment, four per cent. interest is enough in this country to induce the sale of bonds, Mr. Low and Mr. Chittenden can judge better than I.

Adjourned to Thursday morning, April 4, 1878, at half past ten o'clock.

THURSDAY, *April* 4, 1878.

Present, Mr. Buckner, chairman, Messrs. Ewing, Hardenbergh, Hartzell, Bell, Eames, Chittenden, Fort, and Phillips; the Hon. John Sherman, Secretary of the Treasury.

Mr. EWING. I ask your attention to a comparison of the condition of the Treasury for resumption with the condition of the Bank of England in 1819 and now, with the Bank of France this year, and with the banks of the United States in 1857 and 1861.

Secretary SHERMAN. When I said the other day that I thought the condition of the Treasury on the 1st of January next would be as good as the Bank of England, I had not then before me the actual figures or tables, but only spoke from a general knowledge of the facts. Since then I have given the matter a good deal of attention, and I have got some carefully-prepared tables, founded upon late information, giving the exact comparison of the condition of the Bank of England, the Bank of France, the Bank of Germany, the Bank of Belgium, the national banks, and the Treasury. These tables will show that pretty accurately.

[Secretary Sherman handed the tables to the committee, and they are printed in the appendix. The latest statement of the condition of these banks is found in the London Economist of February 23, 1878, and the older statements are found in McCulloch's Dictionary, a standard authority on the subject, on page 117.]

Mr. EWING. I see you have given the figures of the Bank of France in pounds sterling.

Secretary SHERMAN. Yes; they are reduced to pounds sterling. I ought to say, explanatory of the statement which I have submitted, that there are two modes of making up the accounts of the Bank of England; one by dividing them into the bank department and the issue department, while the other is the consolidated statement.

Mr. EWING. How does this statement give it?

Secretary SHERMAN. It gives the consolidated statement—what is called the old form. The consolidated statement is but a combination of the two departments.

Mr. EWING. Still the consolidated statement charges to the bank the reserve on hand, does it not?

Secretary SHERMAN. If there is any material difference; perhaps I had better put it in both forms, because the Economist gives it in both ways. I will give here the table from the Economist:

ISSUE DEPARTMENT.

Notes issued	£38,698,020	Government debt...........	£11,015,100
		Other securities............	3,984,900
		Gold coin and bullion......	23,698,020
	38,698,020		38,698,020

BANKING DEPARTMENT.

Proprietors' capital.........	£14,553,000	Government securities......	£15,203,201
Rest......................	3,414,161	Other securities............	17,672,338
Public deposits, including exchequer, savings banks, commissioners of national debt, and dividend accounts....................	6,524,776	Notes...................... Gold and silver coin........	12,368,965 1,032,773
Other deposits..............	21,529,721		
Seven-day and other bills....	255,619		
	46,277,277		46,277,277

Dated February 21, 1878.

F. MAY,
Chief Cashier.

THE OLD FORM.

The above bank-accounts would, if made out in the old form, present the following results:

Liabilities.		*Assets.*	
Circulation (including bank post-bills)	£26,584,674	Securities....................	£33,322,539
Public deposits	6,524,776	Gold and bullion	24,730,793
Private deposits............	21,529,721		
	54,639,171		58,053,332

The balance of assets above liabilities being £3,414,161, as stated in the above account under the head "Rest."

Now, in regard to the United States, I have a statement here showing the apparent and probable condition of the United States Treasury on April 1, 1878, and on the 1st of January next. The only difference in these statements is that I add to the present condition of the Treasury the proposed accumulation of fifty millions of coin and a substantial payment before that of the fractional currency. I think it will be practically redeemed before that time. The actual results show the amount of demand liabilities on April 1, 1878, against the United States as

$460,527,374, and they show the demand resources, including coin and currency, at $174,324,459, making the percentage of resources to liabilities 37. To show the probable condition of the Treasury on the first of January, 1879, I add the fifty millions of coin and I take off the fractional currency, and deduct estimated United States notes lost and destroyed, leaving the other items about the same. That would show an aggregate of probable liabilities of $435,098,400 and probable cash resources of $224,324,459, making 51 per cent. of the demand liabilities. The ratio of the Bank of England, at this time, is 45 per cent.; the ratio of the Bank of France is 65 per cent.; the ratio of the Bank of Germany is 58 per cent.; and the ratio of the Bank of Belgium is 25 per cent., all based upon the same figures. (See Appendices 7 and 8.)

Mr. EWING. Does not this statement charge to the Bank of England the unissued notes?

Secretary SHERMAN. No, sir; not at all. The notes on hand in the banking department are deducted from the notes issued, so that the circulation in the consolidated statement shows an aggregate of £26,584,674.

Mr. EWING. Does that include the amount of notes unissued?

Secretary SHERMAN. No, sir; the total amount of circulation, as shown by the issue department, is £38,698,020; but there is in the banking department some twelve millions of pounds. This statement deducts the notes on hand from the notes issued (which is proper), and gives the actual notes to be provided for at £26,584,674.

Mr. EWING. Is there not some error about that?

Secretary SHERMAN. Neither you nor I want to fall into any error about this; but my understanding is, that the whole amount of notes of the Bank of England issued by the issue department is £38,698,020; but the banking department has on hand £12,368,965, and in stating the amount of notes outstanding, they deduct that twelve millions from the thirty-eight millions, which ought to be done, because the twelve millions really belong to the Bank of England. Now, in stating ours we have done it differently. We have given the full aggregate without deducting the notes on hand, so that the account is more favorable to the Bank of England as thus stated than it is to us. If I am mistaken about this, I shall be very glad indeed to have you point it out, but I think I am not, because I have looked very carefully into it.

In regard to the national banks, here are some statements which are interesting to me and which were prepared in consequence of our interview the other day. I think they will be interesting to the committee. The first paper contains the circulation and deposits and specie of the State banks in 1857 and 1860, as compiled from statements in the finance report of 1876, pages 204 and 205. The next paper contains the circulation, deposits, and cash reserve of the national banks on the 28th day of December, 1877. The latest statement of the banks I cannot give you, because it is not yet made up. It was made in March last, and the returns are not fully in. This statement shows a general demand liability of $960,816,052, and it shows a total cash reserve of $145,019,338. The ratio of legal-tender funds to the amount of circulation is 48.4 per cent. The ratio of legal-tender funds to circulation and deposits is 15.1 per cent. The next paper exhibits the circulation, deposits, and cash resources of the national banks on December 28, 1877, on a different basis, counting the amount of national bonds owned by the banks and deposited with the Treasurer as money. This other table excludes them entirely. This gives the same figures, but counting the bonds at their nominal par as money, it shows this result: Total amount of liabilities $960,816.052, and total amount of cash resources (including four hundred and five millions of bonds) at $550,201.055. The ratio of cash resources to circulation is 183 per cent. and the ratio of cash resources to circulation and deposits is 57 per cent. (See Appendix No. 6.)

Mr. EWING. Do you think that the bonds can be counted as cash?

Secretary SHERMAN. Yes; the bonds are all worth par or above in gold.

The CHAIRMAN. The other cash held by the banks is legal-tender notes?

Secretary SHERMAN. Yes, and coin.

Mr. EWING. Do you think it safe to count these bonds as gold? Is it possible to convert them into gold?

Secretary SHERMAN. O, yes.

Mr. EWING. That is, the banks can sell over four hundred millions of bonds and get gold for them?

Secretary SHERMAN. Probably not to-day or in a moment.

Mr. EWING. At any time can the national banks accumulate four hundred millions of gold by sale of their bonds?

Secretary SHERMAN. Not in a day.

Mr. EWING. Or in a year?

Secretary SHERMAN. O, yes. I sold last year (within the year) of 4½ per cent. and 4 per cent. bonds two hundred and seventy-five million dollars.

Mr. EWING. How much gold did you get for them?

Secretary SHERMAN. Sixty or seventy millions of gold and the balance I paid for six per cent. bonds.

Mr. EWING. They were practically funded in other bonds. But I want to know now if you make up that table on the theory that these four hundred millions of bonds can be turned into gold for the purpose of resumption?

Secretary SHERMAN. I make up my statement on the theory that four hundred millions of bonds will more than pay four hundred millions of bank-notes at any time, such bonds as the banks hold, and that, if that is not so, we are bankrupt. I just give you this statement. Here also is an abstract of reports made to the Comptroller of the Currency, because these tables are taken from it. (See appendix No. 6.)

Mr. EWING. Here is a consolidated statement which I have prepared, and to which I wish to call your attention.

MR. EWING'S TABLE.

THIS TABLE RELATES TO NO OTHER BANKS THAN BANKS OF ISSUE.

	Currency outstanding.	Deposits.	Total circulation and deposits.	Coin and bullion in the banks.	Estimated specie in the country.	Authority.
Bank of England, December, 1877	$133,950,000	$131,000,000	$265,550,000	$120,150,000	} $772,000,000	London Economist's "Commercial History and Review of 1877." The specie deposits of the English country banks are unknown. The estimate as to the coin and bullion in Great Britain in 1875 was made by the deputy master of the British mint. (See Spofford's American Almanac, 326.)
English country banks, 1877	25,000,000					
Scotch and Irish banks	67,500,000					
Bank of England, 1818	130,000,000	32,000,000	162,000,000			Tooke's History of Prices, and Mushet's Inquiry into the Effects of Bank of England Issues. Palgrave's Notes on Banking says the amount of coin in England in 1819 was £10,000,000. The Bank paid out in 1821–'22 £12,000,000, and increased its stock from £3,400,000 in August, 1819, to £10,000,000 in August, 1822. Probable stock, $150,000,000.
English country banks, 1818	102,000,000					
Bank of England, 1822	87,225,000	18,000,000	105,225,000		50,000,000	
English country banks, 1822	40,350,000				150,000,000	
American banks, 1837	149,185,890	127,397,000	276,582,890	37,915,300	60,000,000	Report of Comptroller of the Currency, 1876. Mr. Webster's Speeches on the Currency, 1838. The excess of specie imported over that exported, between 1837 and 1843, was $30,000,000.
American banks, 1843	58,563,608	56,168,000	114,731,603	33,515,800	90,000,000	
American banks, 1857	214,351,000	230,350,000	444,701,000	58,349,006	240,000,000	Report of Comptroller of the Currency, 1876. Fawcett's Gold and Debt.
American banks, 1858	155,208,000	185,932,000	341,140,000	74,412,800	235,000,000	Report of Comptroller of the Currency, 1876. Amasa Walker.
American banks, 1861	202,000,000	257,229,000	459,229,000	87,674,000		
Bank of France, December, 1877	487,100,000	134,200,000	621,300,000	417,400,000	1,400,000,000	London Economist. Victor Bonnet's "Two Essays." French custom-house returns.
Imperial Bank of Germany, December, 1877	161,650,000	3,900,000	*236,000,000	129,850,000	700,000,000	London Economist. Fawcett's Gold and Debt.
American banks and Treasury, 1878	643,000,000	614,822,000	†1,257,822,000	†147,000,000	264,990,000	Official reports. Dr. Linderman's estimate (appendix to this volume, No. 9).

* In this total of $236,000,000 are *not* included the deposits either of the Imperial or the other issuing banks of the Empire, of which latter there are thirty-two, but the average aggregate note circulation of all the banks, Imperial and local.

† This aggregate of $147,000,000 includes the coin held by the banks and bankers east of the Rocky Mountains, but does not include the subsidiary silver in the banks.

Secretary SHERMAN [examining the paper]. Your currency outstanding of the Bank of England is about what I have got it, about twenty-six million pounds; but yours is made up only to December, 1877, and mine is made up to February. I have no doubt that you have got this correct. There is no trouble about these figures, although we may sometimes look at them a little differently.

Mr. EWING. I cannot get the deposits in the English country banks.

Secretary SHERMAN. The great liability of the Bank of England is the deposits. I have no doubt that this table is substantially taken from the same authority, and I should like to have it go into the report of the conference as yours.

Mr. EWING. I wish you to state the probable amount of gold and silver, not including subsidiary coin, in the United States, outside of national banks and of the Treasury, and where it is or supposed to be.

Secretary SHERMAN. I am like you and like everybody else as to my knowledge on that subject. I have to depend upon the information from the Director of the Mint for it, and I can only give it to you as he gives it. This table here [handing it to the committee] gives that information from the best lights I can get, and I am inclined to think on the whole that it is about right, but I give it as the statement of the Director of the Mint, for I have no knowledge outside of that which I get from him and from the official documents.

[The paper, being an estimate of the amount of gold and silver bullion and coin in the United States on April 1, 1878, is published in the appendix No. 9, giving the total at $199,490,753 of gold and $65,500,000 of silver, making an aggregate in gold and silver of $264,000,000.]

Secretary SHERMAN. That statement is not only concurred in by Dr. Linderman, who has mainly prepared it, but it has been carefully examined by other officers of the Treasury Department who are familiar with the matter.

Mr. EWING. Have you with you the report of the sinking fund ?

Secretary SHERMAN. In my report I refer to the sinking fund. I say: "In the last annual report my predecessor stated that had the resources of the Treasury during each fiscal year, commencing with 1862, been sufficient to make a literal compliance with the conditions of the sinking-fund law practicable, a total of $433,848,215 would have been applied to that fund July 1, 1876; whereas the actual reduction of the debt, including accrued interest, less cash in the Treasury at that date, amounted to $658,992,226," or $220,954,459 in excess of the amount required by law to be provided for that fund. The details of the fund are given on pages 19–20 of my report.

Here is a table showing the excess or deficiency placed each year in the sinking fund since 1869 :

Excess or deficiency placed each year in sinking fund, since 1869.

	Excess.	Deficiency.	Difference.
1869	$672,020 23		
1870		$744,711 80	
1871		257,474 32	
1872	2,823,891 46		
1873	1,451,588 95		
1874		16,305,421 96	
1875		5,996,039 62	
1876		1,143,769 82	
1877		9,225,146 63	
	4,947,500 64	33,672,564 15	
			$28,725,063 51

Here is also a table showing the

Monthly redemptions of legal-tenders and fractional currency during the current fiscal year, to be applied to the sinking fund.

	Legal-tenders.	Fractional currency.
July, 1877	$670, 112	$618, 801 45
August, 1877	1, 118, 056	612, 221 50
September, 1877	1, 061, 232	385, 472 12
October, 1877	2, 424, 040	434, 067 61
November, 1877	3, 150, 604	309, 554 14
December, 1877	1, 396, 512	278, 911 62
January, 1878	833, 352	292, 189 18
February, 1878	492, 400	281, 221 58
March, 1878	769, 312	240, 582 52
Total for 1878	11, 915, 620	3, 453, 021 72
Amount applied to the sinking fund during the fiscal year 1876	5, 999, 296	7, 062, 142 09
Amount applied to the sinking fund during the fiscal year 1877	10, 007, 952	14, 043, 458 05
Total	27, 922, 868	24, 558, 621 86

Now I want to show you also that the surplus revenue has not been equal to the sinking fund since 1874; but actually there has been more applied to the sinking fund than the surplus revenue during those years.

My report of December 3, 1877, will show the exact application of the amount. The amount of the surplus revenue is stated there at $30,340,577, which was applied as follows:

To the redemption of United States notes, &c $10,071,617
To the redemption of fractional currency............................... 14,043,458
To the redemption of 6 per cent. bonds for the sinking fund 447,500
To increase of cash balance in the Treasury 5,778,002

30,340,577

That $5,778,002 has never been applied.

Mr. EWING. Is that thirty millions the sum of the sinking fund?

Secretary SHERMAN. It is the sum of the surplus revenue, the total revenue over expenditures. So that that five millions has not been applied.

Mr. EWING. Where do you expect to get the additional fifty millions of gold by January 1, 1879?

Secretary SHERMAN. You must see that for me to state too closely what I propose to do might prevent me from doing what I expect to do, and therefore I will answer your question just as far as I think you will say I ought to go. I answer, mainly from the sale of bonds. Indeed, in the present condition of the revenue, we cannot expect much help from surplus revenue, except so far as that surplus revenue may be applied to the payment of greenbacks and to the redemption of fractional currency in aid of the sinking fund. To that extent I think we can rely upon revenue enough to retire the United States notes redeemed under the resumption act; so that I would say that we can get the $50,000,000 of gold additional by the sale of bonds. As to the kind of bonds that I would sell, and as to how I would sell them, &c., I ought not to say anything on that subject at present, because you ought to allow me as an executive officer, in the exercise of a very delicate discretion, free power to act as I think right at the moment, holding me responsible for my action afterward. As to what bonds I will sell, or where I will sell them, or how I will sell them, as that is a discretionary power left with the Secretary, I ought not to decide that now, but to decide it as the case arises.

Mr. EWING. I understood you to say in your interview with the Senate committee that you would have to rely upon the natural currents of trade to bring gold from abroad; that is, that there cannot be a large sale of bonds for coin abroad. Is it on a foreign sale that you are relying?

Secretary SHERMAN. Not at all, but on a sale at home. Perhaps I might as well say that if I can get two-thirds of this year's supply of gold and silver, it will amount to a good deal more than $50,000,000, so that I do not have to go abroad for gold. If we can keep our own gold and silver from going abroad, it is more than I want.

The CHAIRMAN. For this $50,000,000 additional I suppose you rely to some extent on the coinage of silver?

Secretary SHERMAN. To some extent; silver and gold we consider the same under the law.

Mr. EWING. Do you expect to pay out the silver dollar coined by you for current expenses, or only for coin liabilities, or to hoard it for resumption?

Secretary SHERMAN. I expect to pay it out now only in exchange for gold coin or for silver bullion. I am perfectly free to answer the question fully, because on that point, after consulting with many members of both houses, I have made up my mind what the law requires me to do. I propose to issue all the silver dollars that are demanded in exchange for gold coin. That has been going on to some extent; how far I cannot tell. Then I propose to use the silver in payment for silver bullion, which I can do at par in gold. I then propose to buy all the rest of the silver bullion which I need under the law with silver coin. As a matter of course, in the current course of business, some of that silver coin will go into circulation; how much, I do not know. The more, the better for us. But most of it, I take it, will be transferred to the Treasury for silver-certificates (that seems to be the idea of the bill), and those silver-certificates will come into the Treasury in payment of duties, and in that way, practically, the silver will belong to the government again.

Until silver is so abundant that it becomes the acknowledged basis of coin transactions, we cannot pay out that silver for the ordinary expenses of the government, because we have not enough to pay all the expenditures in silver; and if the silver is maintained at par with gold, and if the United States notes are below par with gold, we cannot discriminate in favor of any class of creditors; we would, therefore, have to hold silver at par with gold until we either have enough to pay everything with it or until the legal-tender notes are practically at par with gold and silver. That is a matter over which I have no more control than any other citizen. The silver dollars being receivable for duties—the law allowing them to be converted into certificates which are receivable for customs—I must receive them; and I could not prevent, if I tried, the silver from coming into the Treasury, either for silver certificates or payment of duties. As to when I shall commence paying them out for the current expenditures of the government or in payment of the interest or principal of the debt I cannot tell, because that would depend upon the equality of the three kinds of currency—gold, silver, and paper. I do not know whether I make myself understood, but that is the general idea I have in my mind. As a matter of course, it being a great discretionary power which you have invested in the office of Secretary of the Treasury, while I hold the office I will be very careful to exercise that power so as to carry out in good faith the law as Congress has passed it, and that law, I think, contemplates that gold, silver, and paper shall be all brought on an equivalency.

Mr. EWING. Please state in detail the fund in the Treasury, other than gold and silver, applicable to resumption, and not covered by appropriations.

Secretary SHERMAN. It is very small. In round numbers, the $70,-000,000 of currency in the Treasury, which is less than the average amount so held for the last five years, is subject to the following, viz:

Special fund for redemption of fractional currency	$10, 000, 000
Redemption of notes of national banks "failed," in "liquidation," and "reducing circulation"	12, 000, 000
Five per cent. redemption fund	9, 000, 000
Disbursing officers' balances	13, 000, 000
Certificates of deposit issued under act June 8, 1872	26, 000, 000

So that, you may say, some of those items are ours. First, the item of $10,000,000 for the redemption of fractional currency is ours; then the item of $13,000,000, held by disbursing officers, is ours. The two redemption funds, one of national banks that have failed, and the other in -present redemption of national-bank notes (together $21,000,000), belong to the banks. We have to hold it, but the amount does not vary much. The certificates of deposit are less now than usual; they are only $26,000,000. I think that answers your question fully. (See Appendix No. 11 as to distribution of currency in the Treasury.)

Mr. EWING. No; what I desire to know is the funds in the Treasury other than gold und silver applicable to resumption, and not covered by appropriations.

Secretary SHERMAN. I do not count any of these as applicable to resumption.

Mr. EWING. You spoke the other day about $70,000,000 in the Treasury with which to maintain resumption.

Mr. SHERMAN. Not to redeem notes. That $70,000,000 is so much money that is almost constantly in our hands, and which cannot be presented for redemption. In that view only I spoke of it.

Mr. EWING. You did not speak of it, then, as a fund available for use in maintaining resumption?

Secretary SHERMAN. O, not at all; but as so much money which cannot be presented for redemption.

Mr. EWING. Cannot the $26,000,000 of certificates of deposit be presented for redemption?

Secretary SHERMAN. Yes; that much can be; but it is not likely to be. We have got the money to pay for it if it is presented, but it is not likely to be.

Mr. EWING. That depends upon the preferences of the holders of the certificates.

Secretary SHERMAN. Still, I can tell you that it is a great comfort to have $70,000,000, where it is not likely to be disturbed.

The CHAIRMAN. You are not liable to be called for it at any day?

Secretary SHERMAN. No, sir.

Mr. EWING. Then I understand that you have no right to use the special fund for the redemption of fractional currency?

Secretary SHERMAN. I do not think that we have any right to use any of that to redeem notes with, because we must redeem notes with coin; but, having this $10,000,000 on hand, it is ours.

Mr. EWING. Is it subject to use?

Secretary SHERMAN. It is pledged in law to redeem the fractional currency which is really lost or destroyed. If I have $1,000 belonging to a man who died without heirs I am pretty likely to fall heir to it; and that is the case with this special fund for the redemption of fractional currency.

Mr. EWING. What I desire to know is, not what the Treasury might be authorized by additional legislation to do for the purpose of resumption, but the resources of the Treasury under existing laws in legal-tender notes or bank notes that may be used in facilitating resumption. What are the items?

Secretary SHERMAN. I think that practically none of this fractional-currency money and none of this money on hand is available for resumption in the sense in which you use the term. It only lessens the burden of resumption to have the notes where they are not likely to be presented.

Mr. EWING. You certainly spoke the other day of this $70,000,000 as being a resource.

Secretary SHERMAN. I think it is, in this way: It is a resource, because it is like the notes of the Bank of England that are in the issue department. They do not have to be redeemed, or they are not likely to be redeemed, although they may have been issued. They diminish—to the extent that we hold these greenbacks in the Treasury—the amount of greenbacks outstanding among the people.

Mr. EWING. What has been the amount of sales of bonds per month since the last sales to the syndicate?

Secretary SHERMAN. Here it is:

Subscriptions received for four per cent. bonds per month since the last sales to syndicate

January, 1878	$2,846,550
February, 1878	744,200
March, 1878	1,445,450
	5,036,200

Mr. EWING. Then it would take four or five months of sales of bonds to meet outstanding called bonds?

Secretary SHERMAN. We will probably sell enough this month to meet the outstanding called bonds. I think we will be able to sell enough to cover the deficiency in the last call. I hope within this month to make an arrangement to sell, unless Congress should repeal the resumption act. I would like Congress to determine that. If it is not repealed I would undoubtedly sell, during the present month, a good deal more bonds. I would sell all the bonds that I wanted to sell.

Mr. EWING. Four per cent. bonds?

Secretary SHERMAN. That I cannot say. I will do the best I can. I would rather sell four per cent. bonds, and hope to do so; but if I sell any other bonds they will be sold at a premium. I can sell them in the market at above par.

Mr. EWING. Do you think that under existing law the legal-tender notes redeemed will be subject to be paid out as other funds returned to the Treasury?

Secretary SHERMAN. I think that the law is very clear that the amount of legal-tender notes redeemed in excess of $300,000,000 cannot be paid out. That is my construction of the law.

Mr. EWING. I am speaking of the others, and not those redeemed by the increase of bank currency.

Secretary SHERMAN. I do not think they can be issued. I think that those which are redeemed after the 1st of January, in excess of

$300,000,000, cannot bo reissued under existing laws. I am not certain about it. It is a mooted queston; I would rather have your opinion on that than my own. It is a question which I would like very well to have Congress settle. The law proposes and provides for no mode of redeeming United States notes, except as bank-notes are issued (when eighty per cent. of United States notes must be redeemed). As the law provides for no other mode of canceling and destroying United States notes, it would seem to follow that all notes redeemed in any other way than under that law can be reissued, because the section of the Revised Statutes I mentioned provides that all notes which come into the Treasury may be reissued. But then, on the other hand, there is a provision in the resumption law which seems to contemplate that the amount outstanding on the 1st of January shall not exceed $300,000,000.

Mr. EWING. Provided the increase of bank currency is such as to bring down the legal-tender notes to $300,000,000.

Secretary SHERMAN. There is the. question. That question I have never determined in my own mind. It may be that all the notes now outstanding, and which are not redeemed under the provisions of the resumption act, can be reissued.

Mr. EWING. If any can bo they all can be, I think.

Secretary SHERMAN. That is a question I have not determined in my own mind. I have no doubt of my power to reissue all below $300,000,000. The law expressly provides for that; there is no provision of law which authorizes the reducing of them below $300,000,000. But the resumption act does contemplate the reduction of United States notes to $300,000,000.

Mr. EWING. Provided the bank currency is increased to such an extent as, under the provisions of that law, will reduce the greenback currency to $300,000,000.

Secretary SHERMAN. I frankly say that I wish and hope that that is the proper construction; for I do not want to retire greenbacks except as they are retired by the issue of bank notes, because I believe that that process will reduce them in time. I do not desire to hasten the process. But, as a matter of course, I would be very glad indeed if Congress would solve that question for me, just as I would like to have Congress solve the doubt which rests on the reissue of the $300,000,000.

Mr. PHILLIPS. You cancel legal-tender notes to the extent of eighty per cent. of the amount of national bank notes issued, but when these national bank notes are retired (as they have been to a far greater extent than they have been reissued) there is no means in law of reissuing legal-tender notes to that extent.

Secretary SHERMAN. The authority to reissue extends to every dollar of United States notes outstanding. Any of the United States notes that come into the Treasury in the ordinary course of business, either for redemption or in payment of taxes, I have the right to reissue.

Mr. PHILLIPS. That I understand.

Secretary SHERMAN. Then the question is whether that provision of the resumption act which contemplates the reduction of the volume of United States notes to $300,000,000 is a mandate to the executive officer not to reissue them until they fall below that amount. That is a question which I ought not to answer, because I have not made up my mind upon it.

Mr. EWING. But as to the legal-tender notes under $300,000,000, redeemed under the resumption law, you hold that you have the right to pay them out the same as any other fund in the Treasury.

Secretary SHERMAN. I do.

Mr. EWING. You have no more discretion respecting their reissue than you have respecting the reissue of notes received from taxes?

Secretary SHERMAN. No, sir; I issue them according to the exigencies of the public service. Still, you know that that is a disputed proposition. I know a very able Senator, for whose opinion I have great respect, who thinks differently. I think, therefore, that that is a question which Congress ought to settle.

Mr. EWING. Did any law-officer of the government, or any Secretary of the Treasury, give a written opinion to the effect that the authority given to the Secretary of the Treasury by the resumption law to use any surplus revenue from time to time in the Treasury, not otherwise appropriated, to prepare and provide for the resumption of legal-tenders, affects in any way the obligation imposed by that section of the Revised Statutes which declares that the coin paid for customs shall be set apart as a special fund, and applied, first, to the interest on the public debt, and, second to the sinking fund?

Secretary SHERMAN. No; I think that no law-officer of the government, or no Secretary of the Treasury, has yet authoritatively decided that question, as you put it now. The question which the Secretary of the Treasury did decide was, that United States notes and fractional notes, being a part of the public debt, may be included in the sinking-fund; and practically we have paid the full amount of the surplus revenue in that way and applied it to the sinking fund until last year. In one year, in Mr. Bristow's time, there was a deficiency of $5,000,000; and this last year I did not buy bonds to the extent of $5,000,000 of the surplus fund, so that the question which you now present, although it is presented to my mind very often, has not been decided, either by myself or by any Secretary of the Treasury or by any law, for the question has really never been presented in a way which made it necessary to decide it. My annual report will show the exact application of the amount of the surplus revenue. As, under the provisions of existing law, I was actually selling bonds under the resumption act, I did not see my way clear to go into the market and buy these bonds for the sinking fund, just as, during the whole of the war, the sinking-fund provision was held to be inoperative. While we were actually selling bonds, it was absurd for us to go into the market and buy bonds. The money lies in the treasury, subject to the order of Congress. If Congress directs that that $5,000,000 be applied to the sinking fund, it can do so, but it will only involve us in the same absurdity that the English were involved in when they undertook to carry out Sir William Pitt's sinking-fund law during their war.

Mr. EWING. But you can buy 6 per cent. bonds with it, and you can sell 4 per cent. bonds.

Secretary SHERMAN. I know that. We can sell 4 per cent. bonds, but what is the use of doing so?

Mr. EWING. What is the balance for the sinking fund?

Secretary SHERMAN. Five million seven hundred and seventy-eight thousand dollars.

Mr. EWING. Where is that—in the Treasury?

Secretary SHERMAN. It is in the general cash balance. It is in the coin accumulated. Mr. Bristow, in his report in 1875, mentions this very matter, and says that, in his opinion, the law requires him to call in bonds, and to invest this money; but Congress took no action upon it, and the result was that that year, or the preceding year, the balance over the surplus revenue, some $16,000,000, was not applied at all; and so, ever since the panic of 1873, there has been a balance not applied.

Mr. Ewing. I don't think the surplus revenue has anything to do with it; what I wanted to know was whether any law-officer of the government, or any Secretary of the Treasury, had given a written opinion that the sinking fund was to be composed merely of surplus revenue under that section of the Revised Statutes which says that the income from customs shall be applied, first to the interest on the public debt, and second to the sinking fund.

Secretary Sherman. I can only say to you that established custom, as well as the theory of our government, would seem to require that any sinking fund provided for the extinguishment of the debt cannot be applied until after all current demands upon the Treasury are paid. Otherwise, the Treasury would be bankrupt whenever there was a temporary falling off in the revenue. For instance, the law which you read to me and which I helped to frame (the law of 1862), providing for the sinking fund, sets aside the receipts from customs to pay 1 per cent. of the debt. Now, although that was the law, just as mandatory as you have read it (requiring the sinking fund to be maintained at 1 per cent.), the sinking fund was never opened, nor could it be, during the war. The pledge was never carried out until the old floating debt was mainly refunded.

Mr. Ewing. That was covered by the blanket of war necessity.

Secretary Sherman. Not at all. That matter was presented to Congress frequently on the ground that it was impossible to maintain a sinking fund until there was an excess of revenue over expenditure, and so it continued until I myself complained of it, after the war was over, insisting that while that was right during the war, it should not apply after peace, and we, therefore, carried through Congress a provision for the sinking fund, so that the money might be applied, so much every year, in pursuance of the old act of February, 1862, and so it continued to be carried out until the revenues fell below the expenditures, so as to make it impossible to pay the current expenses of the government, and to pay the sinking fund at the same time. Thus, from the necessity of the case, any Secretary of the Treasury was compelled to pay the current demands on the revenue before he paid the sinking fund, just as the manager of a railroad would be bound to pay his hands and furnish the fuel to run his locomotives before he would pay the interest on the first bonded debt.

Mr. Ewing. Was not the public debt being reduced all that time?

Secretary Sherman. Up to the panic of 1873 it was being reduced all the time, and we paid more during all those years than the law required on what we call the sinking fund—that is, the redemption of the debt.

Mr. Phillips. From what source did the payments come?

Secretary Sherman. From surplus revenues. And so it continued until 1873. Then, all at once, there was a deficiency of $16,000,000. Well, the Secretary of the Treasury, as a matter of course, would go on and pay the ordinary expenses first; and if there was any deficiency, he would report that deficiency to Congress, and if there was any fault about it, it was with Congress, for Congress should either provide additional revenues to keep up the sinking fund or else should reduce appropriations. Mr. Richardson was Secretary of the Treasury when the first trouble took place. The exact condition of the Treasury was given two months after the panic, and so on by every Secretary, and as Congress did not feel disposed (and I think rightfully—I was in Congress myself at the time, and take my share of the responsibility) to levy new taxes upon the people in a time of great distress, this deficiency in the sinking fund was allowed to continue from year to year until now, and I presume that it will be allowed to continue, although if Congress can see its way clear to levy a tax upon tea and coffee, to make good the sinking fund, I would like it very much. But I do not think Congress will do so.

Mr. EWING. I guess not.

Secretary SHERMAN. Because I do not think that the people would sustain Congress in it. So I do not think there can be any just criticism in throwing on the sinking fund the actual deficiency in revenue, because any Secretary of the Treasury who would undertake to refuse to pay the current expenses of the government, and who would at the same time pay the whole amount of this technical sinking fund in the purchase and payment of the debt, would be overhauled very quickly.

Mr. EWING. I understood you to say on Monday that this appropriation in the resumption law, of any surplus revenue, authorized you to use any of the funds which would otherwise go to the sinking fund.

Secretary SHERMAN. Yes, for the redemption of United States notes and fractional currency, but not beyond that; I never claimed that.

Mr. EWING. For the redemption of the United States notes after the 1st of January.

Secretary SHERMAN. No, sir; we did not discuss that. The point you were putting to me was that we ought not to have used this money (which should go into the sinking fund) for the purpose of redeeming the United States notes and fractional currency, but that we ought to have applied it to the redemption of bonds; and I said in reply that the plain mandate of the resumption act requiring us to pay and cancel and retire the greenback notes was just as mandatory as the appropriations for your salary and mine.

Mr. EWING. Do I understand you now that the appropriation of "any surplus funds in the Treasury not otherwise appropriated," contained in the resumption law, will authorize you, after the 1st of January, 1879, to use funds which would otherwise go to the sinking fund in redemption of United States notes?

Secretary SHERMAN. My impression is that, under the resumption act, after the 1st of January, I can use all surplus revenue to pay any lawful demands on the Treasury of the United States.

Mr. EWING. That is, it gives you the command of the sinking fund for that purpose?

Secretary SHERMAN. Yes. If Congress fails to make enough appropriation for paying the current expenses, including any demand that may grow out of resumption, I would have a right, to the extent of the surplus revenue, to command those moneys, in order to carry out the resumption act, just as I would have a right to use it under any other act of Congress.

Mr. EWING. So that the sinking fund is not only subordinated to any subsequent appropriations by Congress, but is subordinated to this appropriation in the resumption law of the surplus funds, and is really the last thing which is to be looked after or provided for?

Secretary SHERMAN. Yes; for this reason : if I should fail to have money enough to meet the demands upon me for resumption purposes I am invested with the power to sell bonds; I would have the authority to go into the market and sell bonds. It would be idle for me to go into the market to sell bonds while I was actually buying bonds for the sinking fund. I would regard a demand made upon the Treasury for United States notes after the 1st of January next just like any other demand for a liability which I was bound to pay, and I can use all the means at my command, including the proceeds of the sale of bonds.

Mr. EWING. And the sinking fund?

Secretary SHERMAN. O, yes. The sinking fund, in my view, is nothing but the surplus of revenue over the expenditures. The nature of the sinking fund has been debated to an extent in folios greater than the folios you have got in this room. It was debated in the English Parliament in the famous Dr. Price controversy, which extended for thirty years, and that was the generally recognized idea of a sinking fund—that it was nothing but an agreement on the part of the law-making power to apply surplus revenues to a certain amount to the reduction of the public debt.

Mr. EWING. Has any law-officer of the government, or the Secretary of the Treasury, given a written opinion to the effect either that the sinking fund is subordinated to the special appropriations or to this general appropriation of surplus funds made in the resumption act?

Secretary SHERMAN. No; I do not think so. I know of none.

Mr. EWING. Has any law-officer of the government, or any Secretary of the Treasury, given a written opinion to the effect that the United States notes or fractional currency redeemed may be charged to the sinking fund?

Secretary SHERMAN. No; because I think that that is so clear that I would not ask for such an opinion. The United States notes and fractional currency have been regarded as a part of the public debt ever since their first issue, and in every statement of the public debt it has been always classified as a part of the public debt. In making up the statement of the sinking fund, you will find that we always included the whole aggregate of United States notes and fractional currency.

Mr. EWING. The law unquestionably requires that; but the law also requires that a sum equal to the interest of the sinking fund shall be applied annually.

Secretary SHERMAN. Yes; that has been done.

Mr. EWING. And if you put into the sinking fund notes that bear no interest, it is impossible to execute that provision for paying interest on the sinking fund?

Secretary SHERMAN. What is the sinking fund? The sinking fund is not the identical bonds that are canceled, destroyed, and burned. The sinking fund is neither the bonds paid and destroyed, nor the notes paid and destroyed. The sinking fund is like many other book accounts that are kept upon our books. It is a certain amount of money, and it is accumulated at the rate of 6 per cent. interest. It does not make any difference from what source the sinking fund comes.

Mr. EWING. If there were 5 per cent. bonds in the sinking fund, would you count interest on them at 6 per cent.?

Secretary SHERMAN. But there are no 5 per cent. bonds in the sinking fund. I fell into the same error the other day. I told you the other day that I thought that the interest was computed as at the rate of the bonds purchased; but, on inquiry, I find that I was mistaken, and that the habit has always been to redeem only the 6 per cent. bonds and to compute uniformly 6 per cent. interest on the whole amount of the sinking fund. The sinking fund heretofore has been always composed either of 6 per cent. bonds, United States notes, or fractional currency redeemed.

Mr. EWING. If you had 7.30 bonds in the sinking fund would you not compute the interest at 7.30, and if you had 4 per cent. bonds would you not compute the interest only at 4 per cent.?

Secretary SHERMAN. No, sir. The identity of the particular security is lost the moment that it is redeemed; and the sinking fund is computed at the rate of 6 per cent., because the 6 per cent. bonds are now available and can be paid off.

Mr. PHILLIPS. In case of the falling off of revenue, do you think that you would probably have to sell gold in hand to meet the current expenses of the government?

Secretary SHERMAN. If so, Congress would be in a very sorry predicament.

Mr. PHILLIPS. I am speaking of your power to resume.

Secretary SHERMAN. If Congress fails to give us money enough to meet its appropriations, we are broke. That is all that there is about it.

Mr. PHILLIPS. You would avail yourself then of the coin in your hands to meet the current expenditures of the government?

Secretary SHERMAN. Undoubtedly; but I cannot presume that our government is going to do that.

Mr. PHILLIPS. I observe that the currency balance on the 1st of April, 1877, was eight millions; a little over half a million on the 1st of this April.

Secretary SHERMAN. The balance now is greater than it was then. After I came into the office I established this fund of ten millions for the redemption of fractional currency. That fund had not been established until after I came in. The actual balance is $10,751,851, including that fund of $10,000,000. Formerly that fund had not been stated according to law.

Mr. PHILLIPS. But that fund had all accrued before this year?

Secretary SHERMAN. No, sir; it had not. It was never stated until after I came into office. It was required to be done under the act, and I thought that its not being done was a failure to comply with the act. I therefore directed it to be done.

Mr. PHILLIPS. That is held in legal tenders, is it not?

Secretary SHERMAN. Yes, sir.

Mr. PHILLIPS. But you stated a little while ago that, of your coin balance in hand, there was five millions that had come from the sinking fund.

Secretary SHERMAN. Here is the law under which that ten-million fund is required to be kept. It is the first section of the joint resolution for the issue of silver coin approved July 22, 1876. It is as follows:

That the Secretary of the Treasury, under such limits and regulations as will best secure a just and fair distribution of the same through the country, may issue the silver coin at any time in the Treasury to an amount not exceeding ten million dollars, in exchange for an equal amount of legal-tender notes; and the notes so received in exchange shall be kept as a special fund separate and apart from all other money in the Treasury, and be reissued only upon the retirement and destruction of a like sum of fractional currency received at the Treasury in payment of dues to the United States; and said fractional currency, when so substituted, shall be destroyed and held as part of the sinking fund, as provided in the act approved April seventeen, eighteen hundred and seventy-six.

Now there is the answer, "Shall be held as a part of the sinking fund."

Mr. EWING. The answer makes against your construction, because *there* is a special provision of law that this non-interest-bearing security, when redeemed, *shall* go into the sinking fund. Why should that be put in the law if it was the law already?

Secretary SHERMAN. It had been done before that and afterward. This simply carries out the same thought and the same idea.

Mr. EWING. That is put in to accomplish a purpose.

Secretary SHERMAN. It is a negative pregnant.

Mr. EWING. It was an entirely unnecessary provision, if those notes so destroyed would necessarily go into the sinking fund.

Now, let me ask your attention again to the table you have given us of the items composing the seventy millions of currency in the Treasury.

That ten millions of a special fund for redemption of fractional currency cannot be used by the Secretary, nor the twelve millions for the redemption of the national-bank notes in liquidation, nor the 5 per cent. redemption fund of nine million dollars, nor the funds for which certificates of deposit are issued to the amount of twenty-six millions. None of those items are in the control of the Secretary for use.

Secretary SHERMAN. The ten millions and the thirteen millions are practically as absolutely paid off as if the amount of the United States notes outstanding were reduced to the amount of twenty-three millions.

Mr. EWING. But that fund of ten millions is not under your control under existing law.

Secretary SHERMAN. It is practically redeemed; it is in the Treasury; it is ours.

Mr. EWING. I am speaking of it as a resource. That cannot be used.

Secretary SHERMAN. I explained that before. It cannot be used to pay notes or anything of that kind, but it is none the less currency, which we do not need to provide for; that is all.

Mr. EWING. And the $12,000,000 held for redemption of national-bank notes in liquidation, that can't be used?

Secretary SHERMAN. No; but that is dead while the bank-notes do not come in. As they come in, they are redeemed.

Mr. EWING. Still, it cannot be used by the Secretary?

Secretary SHERMAN. No, sir; nor need it be redeemed.

Mr. EWING. Nor the 5 per cent. redemption fund nor the certificates of deposit?

Secretary SHERMAN. No, sir.

Mr. EWING. Then, of this $70,000,000, there would be only the $13,000,000 to the credit of disbursing officers, which the Secretary is at liberty to use?

Secretary SHERMAN. I would have to make the same explanation which I made in the beginning—that I do not regard the $70,000,000 as a fund on hand with which to redeem anything; but that it is $70,000,000 in hand which is not likely to be called for in coin, and that it lessens, to that extent precisely, the burden of resumption.

Mr. EWING. I understand that perfectly; but I want to bring out this fact definitely—that of that $70,000,000 there is but $13,000,000 that may be used (the balance in the hands of disbursing officers), and that the $57,000,000 cannot be used by the Secretary.

Secretary SHERMAN. No; but it is so much money that is locked up in the Treasury not to be redeemed. Therefore, instead of counting $340,000,000 of legal-tender notes liable to redemption, you may deduct the great body of this $70,000,000, just as in the statement of the Bank of England, which deducts from the total amount of notes issued all the notes held in the banking department.

Mr. EWING. I understand that; and with that explanation you admit my statement—that of the $70,000,000 only $13,000,000 can be issued and used by the Secretary of the Treasury under existing law.

Secretary SHERMAN. For the purposes of resumption.

Mr. EWING. For any purpose.

Secretary SHERMAN. We use it for the redemption of outstanding certificates and for the redemption of bank-notes. We pay it out every day. This money is the most active money that we have in the Treasury. We pay it out and receive it every day.

Mr. EWING. But not for any other purpose than that for which it is specially appropriated?

Secretary SHERMAN. It can only be paid for these particular purposes, but it is being paid out every day, and other money coming in its place.

Mr. EWING. Now, you make the amount of bank-notes of banks in liquidation by your statement to the Senate committee $21,000,000 or $22,000,000.

Secretary SHERMAN. I think that that includes not only notes of banks in voluntary liquidation, but of broken banks.

Mr. EWING. I read from your statement before the Senate committee:

On December 31, 1875, the amount was $346,479,756; on December 31, 1877, $321,672,505, and on February 28, 1878, the amount of bank-notes outstanding was $321,989,991; but the amount of bank-notes of banks in existence, not in process of liquidation, was $299,240,475; and the difference between these two sums being the notes of banks in process of liquidation, although the notes are in circulation, yet an equal amount of greenbacks are in the Treasury as a special deposit to redeem them.

That makes the difference between $321,672,505 and $299,240,475— about $22,000,000.

Secretary SHERMAN. I can tell you the explanation of that. I was correct in my statement before the Finance Committee. There are $21,000,000 or $22,000,000 of notes of outstanding banks in process of liquidation, of which $13,000,000 in United States notes is held in the Treasury, and for the balance we hold the bonds of banks that failed as security. The discrepancy, no doubt, is represented by the fact that we have not sold those bonds. I am surprised that we hold as much as $13,000,000 of notes, for we do not usually sell bonds until the proceeds are needed to redeem the outstanding notes of those bonds.

Mr. EWING. When a bank goes into liquidation it deposits greenbacks to redeem its notes.

Secretary SHERMAN. Yes; but failed banks do not. When banks fail we take possession of their bonds and we sell them only as we need the proceeds to meet their notes. I have no doubt that the great body of this $13,000,000 on hand is money deposited by banks which have voluntarily retired. They have to deposit greenbacks before they get their bonds. But in the case of banks that fail, we sell the bonds as we need the proceeds from time to time. That will doubtless explain the discrepancy.

Mr. EWING. That explains why the item is not $22,000,000 instead of $12,000,000.

Secretary SHERMAN. Yes; we can, if we desire, sell all the bonds that we hold as security for those broken banks, but the usual course is not to do so, but to give the stockholders the benefit of their circulation, and only to sell the bonds as money is needed to redeem the bank-circulation.

Mr. EWING. There is a fraction under $300,000,000 of national-bank notes outstanding, but the five per cent. redemption fund is only put down at nine millions; it should be fifteen millions.

Secretary SHERMAN. No; the explanation of that is this: As the notes of banks in operation come in we redeem them, and at the end of ten days, or oftener if the Treasury sees proper, these notes are returned to the banks issuing them, and are replaced by the banks with greenbacks. This redemption of bank-notes for the time diminishes the $15,000,000 or five per cent. fund to some extent, but at the end of ten days the redeemed bank-notes are sent back to the banks and replaced by other United States notes. In other words, there is a little leeway given there in the ordinary course of business.

Mr. EWING. That is only $500 to every bank. That would scarcely make the difference between $9,000,000 and $15,000,000.

Secretary SHERMAN. It will make it. Ten days' redemption makes about $5,000,000.

Mr. EWING. That explains the discrepancy, therefore.

Secretary SHERMAN. Yes; it is always so. Mr. Gilfillan has been of late very strict with the banks.

Mr. EWING. In case of a drain of gold from the Treasury, what measure would you resort to to check it—I mean after resumption?

Secretary SHERMAN. The Treasury ought to be so strong that the thing would check itself. You can scarcely imagine, in the probabilities of business, that, with no outstanding liabilities that are not covered by actual cash on hand except the $300,000,000 of legal-tender notes, the drain upon the government would be so great as to exhaust the reserve of $120,000,000. That proposition is all based, not upon the fact that $120,000,000 would pay $300,000,000—we all know that is not so—but upon the fact that it is impossible to gather together United States notes and to present them in such a mass and in such a continuous stream, and that the very effort to do so would raise the value of United States notes. Their convenience is so great, and the necessity for them so apparent, that such an effort would at once bring them up to par in gold. I think that a drain of five, ten, fifteen, or twenty millions would at once tend to bring up the value of greenbacks until they were at par in gold, and then there would be no object at all in drawing them out.

Mr. EWING. After resumption the greenback must remain at par in gold as long as the Treasury maintains resumption?

Secretary SHERMAN. Certainly; and while they are at par in gold they will not be presented to any considerable extent.

Mr. EWING. Of course, if there was an established difference of 1 per cent., or one-half of 1 per cent., between gold and greenbacks, the Treasury would be broken pretty quick?

Secretary SHERMAN. Yes, sir, or a quarter of 1 per cent.; there is no doubt about that.

Mr. EWING. Therefore, after resumption, greenbacks must necessarily be at par with gold so long as the Secretary is able to maintain resumption? Now, I am supposing a case of a drain of gold from the action of foreign creditors, or from any other cause, and want to know what means you would resort to to check it?

Secretary SHERMAN. I do not think that it would be necessary to resort to any means; but if it were necessary to devise some means, I would resort to such as have been adopted in other countries—the temporary suspension of specie payment. That is a question for Congress. The British bank act, which is so often quoted as the standard, makes no provision for suspension; there is no legal suspension of payment in England, nor does our law make any provision for it. If the government should meet such an adverse state of circumstances as to make suspension absolutely necessary, the government would necessarily have to take the responsibility of it, leaving Congress to determine whether the circumstances justified it. That has always been so.

Mr. PHILLIPS. Then do you think that the Secretary of the Treasury has the power to suspend specie payment?

Secretary SHERMAN. No, sir; but if demands were made upon the Treasury, which the Secretary could not pay unless he was to pay them out of his own pocket, he would have to stop paying. That is all there is about it.

Mr. EWING. When, short of the point of your actual inability to go further, would you feel at liberty to stop?

Secretary SHERMAN. That I cannot state. That will not occur in my time if you give me now such a reserve as I mention, and it will not occur at all, in your time or in my time, in my judgment. But we cannot anticipate what the future will bring forth. We do not know but that we may be involved in war, which would compel a suspension of payment, and we do not know what might be the effect of war in Europe.

Mr. PHILLIPS. I was going to ask you on that very point. Would not a general war in Europe result in raising the price of gold?

Secretary SHERMAN. Wise men differ very much upon that. I think that a general war in Europe would give such a demand for our agricultural products, and for everything that we produce and sell, that it would probably inspire confidence, and there would be less danger.

Mr. PHILLIPS. Might it not raise the price of gold as compared with currency?

The CHAIRMAN. Or might it not have the effect of sending our bonds here?

Secretary SHERMAN. We are not bound to pay for our bonds unless they are due.

Mr. EWING. But banks and others that hold gold would be tempted to buy bonds, and the gold would go out.

Secretary SHERMAN. I do not think so. I have shown you now in these figures that, with such a reserve as I have mentioned, the government of the United States is stronger for resumption than the Bank of England.

Mr. EWING. Is now?

Secretary SHERMAN. No; I say will be, if you give us the reserve I mention. It will then be stronger than the Bank of England.

Mr. EWING. You said on Monday that it is now stronger.

Secretary SHERMAN. I do not think that it is now, but I say that before the 1st of January, with an additional reserve of $50,000,000, and if you will provide enough means to carry on the current expenses of the government, with or without regard to the sinking fund, we will be stronger than the Bank of England. If you make good the sinking fund, we would be better off; but if you do not make it good, it does not affect the question of resumption. With that $50,000,000 additional (making our reserve $130,000,000 or $140,000,000), with the fact that our notes are of universal credit and are distributed throughout this great extent of country and among 40,000,000 of people, with the fact that $70,000,000 of our notes are now in the treasury not likely to be called upon, and with the fact that the banks have to take care of $70,000,000 more, which they cannot run in upon us without subjecting themselves to the violation of the law of their creation, with their notes absolutely secured by United States notes—if we cannot maintain specie payment, then it is impossible to maintain specie payment on a paper circulation.

The CHAIRMAN. That is on the theory all the time that paper and gold are equivalent?

Secretary SHERMAN. Certainly. Specie payment means; the equivalency of gold and paper. It is on the theory that the 1 per cent. difference between gold and silver will disappear before the 1st of January that I propose to commence specie payments; but suppose that I am mistaken; suppose that your fears are well grounded and that I am over sanguine, as some people say I am, still, Congress will meet in December, and then the question will be so apparent to every man that, if the resumption act cannot be carried out, I shall come to Congress and say that I have been unable to accumulate this reserve, or that an adverse state of circumstances has arisen, and that I am unable to do what the resumption act requires of me.

Mr. EWING. But in the mean time the country is on the rack and torture of preparation for impracticable resumption.

Secretary SHERMAN. There you are mistaken. The process toward resumption is not a harsh process. What is harsh, and what has been of great weight upon the people, has been the effect of extreme paper inflation, resulting in the panic of 1873, sixteen or eighteen months before the passage of the resumption act. Last summer, when I accumulated $60,000,000 of gold, and was going on refunding the debt, every sign of prosperity was increasing and business was getting better.

Mr. EWING. In your conference with the Senate committee, you spoke of "this long, weary agony and struggle toward resumption," and I think that the country will agree with you that there is enough of agony in it.

Secretary SHERMAN. Wherever there is an evil caused by inflated money, the instincts of human nature lead men back to specie payment, and the whole process from 1873 down to the present time is a process toward resumption.

Mr. EWING. If the resumption law had never been passed, the country would have revived from the panic of 1873 during the year 1875.

Secretary SHERMAN. You and I, no doubt, differ very honestly on that point.

Mr. HARTZELL. What would be the effect of this resumption act upon the national banks and their depositors?

Secretary SHERMAN. I cannot see that it will have any injurious effect. Wherein?

Mr. HARTZELL. I understand from your statement here last Monday, that the national banks hold $600,000,000 of deposits. Lack? of confidence might induce the depositors to go to these national banks and demand on the 1st of January, or soon after the resumption act takes effect, a large amount of gold.

Secretary SHERMAN. No; United States notes.

Mr. PHILLIPS. Which would command gold.

Mr. HARTZELL. And if the banks did not have them, and the supposition is that they could not——

Secretary SHERMAN. All the national banks in the country have but $70,000,000 of greenbacks.

Mr. HARTZELL. The banks would have to furnish to the depositors either gold or greenbacks, but they could not furnish either to half the amount of their deposits?

Secretary SHERMAN. No, sir.

Mr. EWING. The aggregate of deposits in all the banks, national, State, private, and savings banks, as shown by the report of the Comptroller, is $2,120,000,000.

Secretary SHERMAN (to Mr. Hartzell). Your question is a very proper one. I can only give you my idea. All banking is based upon the idea that a larger amount of paper money can be maintained in circulation than the money in which it is to be redeemed. Otherwise there would be no object in banking. The Bank of England and the small banks of England maintain a cash reserve varying from 9 per cent. up to about 33 or 40 per cent. The Bank of France and the Bank of Germany, which are really government depositories, maintain a large reserve. A reserve of 40 per cent. would be considered a very large reserve. The only answer to your question is that experience has shown, to the satisfaction of the banks, that their deposits will not be all demanded. If they are demanded they will be paid by credits. Most of these depositors are debtors to the banks, as well as creditors of the banks. They are customers. The balance of credits would pay off a good deal of the deposits of the banks, and experience shows that a certain amount of money on hand and available, with a good line of discounts to support it, is sufficient. As to the notes of national banks, every dollar of them is secured by United States bonds to an amount of at least 10 per cent. greater than the amount of notes outstanding; and these bonds are of such universal credit and ready sale that in the ordinary course of business they can be very readily converted into any kind of money.

Mr. EWING. What about the $1,500,000,000 of deposits in other banks than national banks?

Secretary SHERMAN. They are private individual debts; the government has nothing to do with them.

Mr. EWING. The government has certainly to consider them in the plan of resumption?

Secretary SHERMAN. It has to consider them just as it has to consider any other public fact.

Mr. EWING. More than that; they have a direct bearing on the practicability of government redemption, for the legal-tender note is the only paper money redeemable in coin, and on the $348,000,000 of legal-tender notes rest $300,000,000 of national-bank notes and $2,120,000,000 of cash demand deposits. That is all to be considered.

Secretary SHERMAN. It is all to be considered, but $10 will pay $100 of deposits in the ordinary course of business.

Mr. HARTZELL. Does the mere fact that the government will, on the 1st of January, be able to redeem all its legal-tender notes, bring us of itself to specie resumption? Is that what we mean by specie resumption?

Secretary SHERMAN. I mean by specie resumption not the payment of all these debts in coin, but I mean the equivalency of these United States notes with coin, so that the people will take paper at par with coin, and if they want the coin they can get it. I do not suppose that $1 out of $100 of greenbacks will be presented for redemption.

Mr. HARTZELL. The national banks are close corporations, as I understand, and there is a general understanding between them on all questions affecting their interests, as we find by their unanimity in applying for a repeal of the bank-tax.

Secretary SHERMAN. Mr. Chittenden here can tell you that there are no people who have such diverse views as the national banks.

Mr. HARTZELL. If it should appear that the safety and security of these national banks demanded it, could they not unite and get together such securities and present them to the Treasury as would drain the Treasury of all the gold that it has, and thus absolutely prevent, by their combination, the Secretary from carrying out the provisions of the resumption law?

Secretary SHERMAN. I do not think, in the first place, that they would attempt to make such a combination against the government, and, in the second place, I think that if they did it would be very easily met. It is not possible, with the amount of legal-tender notes which they hold—admitted to be about $70,000,000—that they could take the whole of them and present them to the Treasury. Such a thing is not possible, because the banks could not be brought into anything like a co-operation of that kind, nor could they keep up a continuous stream of demand on the Treasury; and then, besides, the Treasury has ample power to make the banks redeem their notes.

Mr. EWING. In legal-tender notes?

Secretary SHERMAN. Yes, in legal-tender notes.

Mr. EWING. Or in silver and gold?

Secretary SHERMAN. Yes; that would throw the gold back on the Treasury. Some of the papers thought that in my remarks the other day I threatened the banks. I did not threaten them, but there is no doubt about it that the Treasury would be stronger than the banks in such a contest. There is no danger that the national banks are going to combine to present their legal-tender notes to the Treasury.

The CHAIRMAN. It would be much more reasonable to suppose that the banks would agree among themselves that their obligations and operations would be in currency, and that their checks would be paid in currency rather than in gold.

Mr. HARTZELL. Suppose that the depositors in the national banks should run in and demand payment of their deposits; would not the national banks be bound to go under?

Secretary SHERMAN. The banks can pay their depositors in greenbacks, because greenbacks are legal tender.

Mr. HARTZELL. How could they when there are only about $220,000,000 of them in circulation?

Secretary SHERMAN. Then, if they cannot get them, how can they present them to us for redemption?

Mr. EWING. They have $70,000,000 which they can present in a week.

Secretary SHERMAN. How can they bring $70,000,000? The national banks in New York, where the largest accumulation of greenbacks is, have only got $11,000,000. I think it is sufficient to say that Mr. Hartzell's supposition is an impracticable one; first, because the banks could have no desire to do such a thing; and, secondly, because it could not be done. It would have to be a very slow operation, and with a reserve of $130,000,000 or $140,000,000 even that extreme danger could be met.

Mr. EWING. In case of an apprehension that the Treasury would have to suspend specie payments, and, consequently, that gold would rise, would not the banks want to convert their reserves, and would they not certainly convert their coin-certificates into gold?

Secretary SHERMAN. It might be; but a suspension of specie payment, or a sudden panic, never comes at a time when people are expecting it or protecting themselves. It always comes like an earthquake, when it is wholly unexpected.

Mr. EWING. You intimated a probability of a suspension by the government, from the running down of the coin in the Treasury.

Secretary SHERMAN. I say that such a thing might be possible.

Mr. EWING. The state of the Treasury is known all the time to the banks and to the public, and certainly the fact that the Treasury was running short of gold would create alarm, and would naturally cause the banks and other holders to precipitate their seventy millions of legal-tender reserves and their fifty-eight millions of gold-certificates on the Treasury.

Secretary SHERMAN. I can only say that the Bank of England has frequently run its gold down—at one time to a million of pounds.

Mr. EWING. Yes, sir; and the bank ran short once and then found a lot of one-pound notes, and they saved it from bankruptcy when gold could not.

Secretary SHERMAN. If you would ever run the Treasury down, so as to redeem the $140,000,000 of the present outstanding legal-tender notes, greenbacks would be so scarce that they would be taken readily by everybody, just as in England, when the bank balance ran down under the panic to one million pounds sterling, every one was anxious to get Bank of England notes. Everybody was eager to get them and to hoard them; so that I do not think this is a danger to be regarded.

Mr. EWING. I want to ask further about your means of stopping a drain. Would you not naturally withhold the greenbacks as they come into the Treasury, in case you became apprehensive at all of a drain of gold?

Secretary SHERMAN. I think I would. If it should so happen that there was a run upon the Treasury for greenbacks, I would not issue them until the run was over.

Mr. EWING. And until the Treasury felt as strong as usual?

Secretary SHERMAN. Yes, sir; and in that event I do not like to say what I would do. I would sell 5 per cent. bonds, if necessary, in an extreme case.

Mr. EWING. In such a contingency the banks would naturally contract their currency also.

Secretary SHERMAN. In case of a panic which would threaten to break the government, or to break the banks, as a matter of course the instinct is one of self-preservation; but that is so whether you have coin payments or currency payments.

Mr. EWING. I am not speaking of a panic, but of the state of the Treasury from time to time. If you find your gold running out, would you not hoard the greenbacks?

Secretary SHERMAN. Naturally; if I found the greenbacks coming in, I would hold on to them until they are called out again in the natural course of business.

Mr. EWING. For the purpose of diminishing the drain on the Treasury of gold?

Secretary SHERMAN. I might temporarily, until that drain passed; but ordinarily I would use them to redeem 6 per cent. bonds.

Mr. EWING. After the drain passed, what would you do?

Secretary SHERMAN. I would pay them out again.

Mr. EWING. That is, you would do very much as the Bank of England does—you would stop the movement of the currency out of the Treasury, as far as practicable?

Secretary SHERMAN. Yes, sir; and, as a matter of course, Congress would be in session from time to time and could be applied to. It may be that Congress may, by future legislation, provide for that contingency.

Mr. EWING. Have you any apprehension that the banks, before resumption day, will present their gold-certificates?

Secretary SHERMAN. I wish they would.

Mr. EWING. That would put a stop to your power to issue certificates to the amount of 20 per cent. beyond the gold on hand.

Secretary SHERMAN. It might, but there is no prospect of that. The power to issue certificates to the extent of 20 per cent. is a power which, up to this time, has not been exercised, and which would not be exercised except in an extreme case. But what motive would the banks have to withdraw the money deposited with us? It is deposited with us for safe keeping, and they would only withdraw it from a fear that it was not safe.

Mr. EWING. Might not the fact that there is a contingency in which you might issue coin-certificates in excess of the coin in the Treasury lead the banks to feel that they had better get their gold ?

Secretary SHERMAN. I do not think so; but at any rate it is safe to say that that thing has not been done, and probably would not be done, except in an extreme emergency, such as would justify the Bank of England in issuing notes when it would not pay gold.

Mr. EWING. Is there not a further reason why the banks would take possession of their gold, when you reach specie payments, which is that they must pay gold when the gold is asked for ?

Secretary SHERMAN. No.

Mr. EWING. Otherwise they will receive no deposits in gold.

Secretary SHERMAN. The banks under the law can always redeem in legal-tender notes.

Mr. EWING. I know that, but if they are to receive deposits in gold they certainly must pay their depositors in gold where the depositors want it. They must treat gold and paper as equivalent exactly, and, therefore, they must have gold on hand to pay those who want gold, otherwise they will not receive a dollar in gold deposits except as special deposits.

Secretary SHERMAN. The fact is that but little gold is paid even on coin payments.

Mr. EWING. But, as a matter of fact, must not the banks have the gold to pay whenever it is demanded ?

Secretary SHERMAN. Yes, sir; on deposits they agree to pay in gold. As a matter of fact, they have some gold to pay now. They have gold in all the city banks, and the reserve of gold in the New York banks is very large; but there is no gold needed in Lancaster or Mansfield, Ohio, where you and I live; what do they need it for ?

Mr. EWING. When you get to specie payments plenty of people will want to hoard it.

Secretary SHERMAN. No; they will hoard silver dollars. The class of people who hoard money are those to whom small sums are great ones.

Mr. EWING. The amount of gold in the banks now is very small, because there is a very small amount of obligations payable in gold; but after resumption day, when you establish that paper and gold and silver are equivalents, a large body of the bank depositors may want gold, and the banks must give gold to their customers who want it. Do you think it necessary to get the amount of legal-tender notes down to $300,000,000 before the 1st of January, 1879, in order to resume with safety ?

Secretary SHERMAN. I would like to have it so, but even if I do not succeed, I would not postpone resumption on that account.

Mr. EWING. In the three and a quarter years since the resumption law was enacted, $35,000,000 of legal-tenders have been drawn in and canceled; is there any probability that, in the time left between now and resumption day, the remaining $47,000,000 can be retired ?

Secretary SHERMAN. No ; I think not.

Mr. EWING. Do you anticipate any considerable reduction of legal-tender notes by the increase of bank currency by next January ?

Secretary SHERMAN. Yes, sir; last month there was a reduction of $1,000,000.   I think that the amount will depend very much on the degree of confidence in the future which prevails in banking circles.

Mr. EWING. That is as to maintaining resumption ?

Secretary SHERMAN. Yes, sir ; that estimate of the amount will be reduced, probably, $1,000,000 a month.

Mr. Ewing. That would leave you with $340,000,000 of legal-tender notes outstanding.

Secretary Sherman. Then I think we can fairly state that this money in the Treasury (that is, the balances held by disbursing officers, the $10,000,000 fund for the redemption of fractional currency, and the money held for the redemption of bank-notes on failed banks) will probably reduce it to the neighborhood of $300,000,000, nominally.

Mr. Ewing. Still that $16,000,000 to disbursing officers goes out.

Secretary Sherman. But there is always about that much on hand.

Mr. Ewing. But I understand that you want to reduce the total volume of legal-tender currency to $300,000,000.

Secretary Sherman. I do.

Mr. Ewing. It is obvious that it cannot be reduced to $300,000,000 on the 1st of January, 1879.

Secretary Sherman. I say it would be better if it could be done; but if it cannot, I would not postpone resumption for that reason, because I think that with this large reserve which I mention we can maintain resumption on the full amount—with the advantage we have of having thirty or forty millions locked up in the Treasury not likely to be used.

Mr. Ewing. Do you think that the balance of trade can be kept in our favor for the next few years?

Secretary Sherman. That is an uncertain problem.

Mr. Ewing. You say, in your Senate interview, that the balance of trade brings us gold and silver and bonds. Has it brought us, in the past few years, gold and silver in excess of the gold and silver exported?

Secretary Sherman. No; you see heretofore silver has been largely exported as bullion, but we received gold, last season, in pretty large sums in this country—precisely how much, I am not prepared to say.

Mr. Ewing. I have here, from the Bureau of Statistics, a statement of the imports and exports of coin and bullion, from 1865 to 1877, which shows a total, for the 13 years, of exports over imports of $692,000,000. (See appendix No. 10.)

Secretary Sherman. Yes, sir; that is so.

Mr. Ewing. That is an average of exports over imports of gold and silver of $53,264,000 a year.

Secretary Sherman. That was at a time when paper money was in universal use, and there was no demand here for silver or gold; but now that we are to have specie payments, that course of things will be naturally expected to cease. You will find it easier to send off the products of our soil than the products of our mines, if we give the same use to the precious metals that is given in other countries.

Mr. Ewing. For the past three years the average excess of the exports of gold and silver, over the imports (the balance of trade being in our favor) has been $42,396,000 a year; and that average is still continuing?

Secretary Sherman. Yes, sir. At this season of the year gold is shipped abroad, and at other seasons of the year it comes back. Sometimes the same gold will flow backward and forward two or three times in the year. After the cotton crop is marketed, and before June, when the canals are open, and products can be moved on the canals, is the time when gold naturally flows abroad, and it comes back in the fall.

Mr. Ewing. Have you any reason to expect that the average exports of bullion, over imports, will not be in excess for the next two or three years as it has been for 17 years past?

Secretary Sherman. I would expect more exports, because of our home products of gold and silver, which may be stated, in round numbers, at $85,000,000. If we can hold two-thirds of it in this country, it is as much as we can expect. That would leave a balance of thirty or forty millions to go abroad. And suppose it does go abroad? We can stand the drain of thirty or forty millions a year, and still have a large amount of gold and silver in this country. (See Appendix No. 12.)

Mr. EWING. Do you not anticipate that drain?

Secretary SHERMAN. I would expect it. Our production of gold and silver is greater than is necessary to maintain resumption in this country, and it will go to help other countries.

Mr. EWING. Will it not go abroad irrespective of our demand for it here?

Secretary SHERMAN. It depends upon whichever demand is the greatest.

Mr. EWING. And upon whoever has the most ability to keep it?

Secretary SHERMAN. Yes, sir.

Mr. EWING. We being the debtor nation, and the people of Europe holding our debts, can they not attract gold from us at present?

Secretary SHERMAN. If we are a debtor nation we are also a nation which the European nations like to have for a debtor. Our nation has been a productive, active nation, and foreign capital seeks a favorite investment here.

Mr. EWING. Still, in case of a want of gold abroad they have it in their power to get it at any time by the sale of our securities.

Secretary SHERMAN. Yes; they can recall it if they want to do so, but the chances are that they will be more likely to invest in our securities in the future than they have been in the past, because this country is a stable country. It has gone through a great civil war, and it has elements of strength and stability which no European country possesses.

Mr. EWING. Our ability to keep gold practically depends upon this, whether our creditors abroad prefer to hold our bonds or to take our gold?

Secretary SHERMAN. Certainly.

Mr. EWING. If they prefer to take our gold they can get it by sending their bonds here and selling them.

Secretary SHERMAN. Yes.

Mr. EWING. And in the past three years, with the balance of trade largely in our favor, the excess of exports of specie over imports has been forty-two millions a year.

Secretary SHERMAN. That is because until last year we have never shown a determination to accumulate coin.

Mr. EWING. Our determination to accumulate coin was as strong in the month of January last as it ever has been, and yet the balance against us in that month was over two million dollars.

Secretary SHERMAN. The cause of the bonds flowing back was the fear of unfriendly legislation. The truth is, that (whether the fear was well or ill founded) a very large amount of our bonds came back which had to be paid in gold or silver because of pending legislation, but that movement has ceased. I got a letter yesterday from the highest authority, stating that that movement of bonds has gradually diminished.

Mr. EWING. Still the export of gold last Saturday was a million and a half of dollars.

Secretary SHERMAN. It always is large at this season of the year. This same gentleman tells me that he does not think that the export of gold this year will be greater than in former years, but that it commenced earlier, caused by the exportation of these bonds from abroad.

Mr. EWING. But the indications are that the excess of shipment of coin will be kept up as compared with the last three years.

Secretary SHERMAN. I hope not at anything like the same rate.

Mr. PHILLIPS. You have stated that you have not been able to ac-cumulate gold at all this year.

Secretary SHERMAN. Yes; because I would not come into competition with the bonds which came back from abroad—caused by the agitation of the silver question.

Mr. PHILLIPS. Can you get coin from 4 per cent. bonds?

Secretary SHERMAN. Not just now to any great extent, but I hope that it will be better, and that I will be able to sell 4 per cent. bonds.

Mr. CHITTENDEN. Will not the mixed condition of the national bank currency be an element of strength in facilitating resumption? For example, if you were to present national bank currency to a bank for redemption, you must separate the notes. If you take any given amount of national bank currency which you find on deposit anywhere, you will be surprised to find how it represents banks from all sections of the country. I take it that no bank can be called upon to redeem any but its own issue.

Secretary SHERMAN. That is so; it is almost impossible to sort national bank bills.

Mr. CHITTENDEN. Will that be for you an element of strength or of weakness?

Secretary SHERMAN. It will be an element of strength. The difficulty of sorting national bank bills is very great. When they come to sort them in the Treasury the bills have to pass through four or five skilled hands. First, they are sorted into States, then into denominations, and then into banks. If you were to try and make a run on any particular bank in this country, as they used to do twenty or thirty years ago, it would be impossible to do so from the difficulty of assorting notes of different banks.

Mr. EWING. The balance of trade in our favor in the past three years has been due not so much to our largely increased exports as to our diminished imports, resulting from diminishing purchasing power.

The total exports for the three years ending June 30, 1874, were....	$1,550,939,000
The total exports for the three years ending June 30, 1877, were....	1,656,201,000
Excess of latter over former period.................................	105,362,000
The total imports for three years ending June 30, 1874, were.........	$1,836,137,000
The total imports for three years ending June 30, 1877, were.........	1,445,069,000
Excess of former over latter period.................................	391,063,000

Now I wish to ask you whether with the removal of the pressure from the country of the threat and preparation for resumption on the 1st of January, 1879, we may not expect that the imports will in-crease, and that we will go back to the old condition of importing more than we export, and in that way increase this drain of gold and silver?

Secretary SHERMAN. I think that the excessive imports for several years before the panic were evidence of the greatest extravagance and disregard of expenditure. People went into debt recklessly. That state of mind is always induced by a superabundance of paper money. I think that one of the best results of the panic (which was bad enough in depressing industry) was in stopping this extravagant and reckless importation of foreign goods. That is an element of real good which has come out of the evil which we have suffered from the past.

Mr. EWING. But you expect to maintain the same volume of paper money, and you expect to add to that volume a considerable amount of specie. That is, you expect to increase the currency as a result of resumption. Certainly, if this condition of extravagance arises from a superabundance of money, that extravagance will be increased very largely after resumption, if your theory be correct.

Secretary SHERMAN. There is a great deal of difference between irredeemable paper money, which fluctuates in value day by day, and redeemable money which always has a coin standard, and is measured by the values of the world. It is not a question of abundance of money so much as it is a question of fluctuations of value. A paper which is irredeemable and fluctuating always induces speculation. For instance, if a man sees that his neighbor has bought a piece of land on which he has made a large profit, he goes into speculation himself; and one man embarks in a hazardous enterprise because another man has done so and has succeeded. Now a redeemable paper money which is always at a fixed standard is less likely to produce that kind of speculative feverish adventure, even although it may be larger in volume.

Mr. EWING. So you understand that with inflation of currency after the 1st of January, 1879, there will not be inflation of values?

Secretary SHERMAN. No; values will be more stable.

Mr. EWING. As a matter of fact, did the greenback currency vary so greatly in purchasing power for the three years before the passage of the act of 1873?

Secretary SHERMAN. O, yes. The purchasing power of the greenback to-day is at least 60 per cent. more than it was before the panic.

Mr. EWING. Undoubtedly, because of the threatened contraction under the operation of the resumption law.

Secretary SHERMAN. No; but because of our getting back to a coin standard.

Mr. EWING. It is because the opinion of the country is that we must submit to an enormous contraction of our paper money, which is the currency with which business is done, in order to reach and maintain resumption.

Secretary SHERMAN. You and I differ about that. I have given you my view. I tell you that I think the falling off of importations is not an unfavorable sign. Every man knows now that money is money, and that he has to earn it. It is an evidence of more stable and economical management of affairs.

Mr. EWING. Do you expect the business of the country to revive after resumption?

Secretary SHERMAN. I think so.

Mr. EWING. Will not the imports increase largely as a necessary result of that revival, and will not, therefore, the balance of trade more likely turn against us by the increase of imports, the present favorable balance being due chiefly to the falling off of imports?

Secretary SHERMAN. I doubt very much whether the importations to this country for many years will equal what they were for the three or four years before the panic. The whole course of our industry has changed within the last three or four years. We are manufacturing now a great many things which we did not manufacture then. We are embarking in a great many industries which did not exist here before the panic. Prices have been reduced so that we can almost compete with any nation, and we export now many articles which we did not think of making until the last few years. When we manufacture upon the basis of a coin standard, like Great Britain and France, we can compete with those nations, because we have over them the great advantage of raw products. To be sure we have the disadvantage of higher-priced labor. Our labor is more intelligent and higher-priced.

The CHAIRMAN. And the disadvantage of higher priced money.

Secretary SHERMAN. Yes; but when we get down to compete with them on the same money, our natural advantages would countervalue the difference in wages and the difference in interest of money. We are now manufacturing a great variety of articles which were never manufactured in this country before. Values now—even gold values—are lower than they were before the panic all over the country. The same amount of money represents now a greater amount of either imports or exports than it did then, because nothing is truer than the fact than that general revulsion which overcame us like a cloud extends all over the civilized world.

Mr. EWING. My belief is that on any revival, any letting up of the pressure caused by the resumption law, the imports will increase relatively to exports, and the old balance of trade will be re established against us, and the drain of gold will return in its full force. (See Appendix No. 13.)

Mr. PHILLIPS. Will not the coin certificates become a part of the currency, when specie payment comes, and so fill up the void made by the retirement of the legal tenders, and probably neutralize the effect of the retirement of the legal-tenders?

Secretary SHERMAN. I think they will; but these coin-certificates are now represented by actual money on hand.

Mr. PHILLIPS. They increase the responsibility of the Treasury just in proportion. They will go into circulation, will they not?

Secretary SHERMAN. Yes. It does not make any difference whether currency is represented by coin-certificates or by actual coin. If they draw out coin, that coin goes into a general circulation, and if they leave it with us, then the certificates go into circulation.

Mr. PHILLIPS. But these coin-certificates will then go into general circulation as they do not go now.

Secretary SHERMAN. Coin-certificates do go into the general circulation for coin purposes now. They are largely used.

Mr. PHILLIPS. But will they not go in for general purposes as circulation?

Secretary SHERMAN. Perhaps they will.

Mr. PHILLIPS. There has been $35,000,000 of legal-tender notes retired under the resumption act?

Secretary SHERMAN. Yes.

Mr. PHILLIPS. Of that amount I have been informed that $15,000,000 has been in small notes; what rule have you to govern the Treasury in that respect?

Secretary SHERMAN. I am glad you mentioned that, because I would like to correct a misapprehension on that point. We always give to every man who makes a demand upon the Treasury any kind of bills he wants. We do not seek to force one-dollar, two-dollar, five-dollar, twenty-dollar, or one hundred-dollar bills. Every person who presents a draft at the Treasury gets the paper money he wants.

Mr. PHILLIPS. But the practical result is that some $15,000,000 of small bills have been retired, to the detriment of small change.

Secretary SHERMAN. Our impression is that that is a mistake.

Mr. PHILLIPS. It has been so stated to me.

Secretary SHERMAN. I can give you the fact exactly. I suppose it is because the banks, to whom the great body of the paper money is paid out, do not wish to handle small bills, and require large ones; but anybody who wants the small bills can have them. I will give the exact amount at different dates, so that you will see how much the circulation of small bills has fallen off. *

Mr. PHILLIPS. Do you think that the proportion of small bills retired has not been much greater than the proportion of large bills retired ?

Secretary SHERMAN. I do not know. I would rather give you the exact figures. General Butler talked to me yesterday about it, and I told him what I say to you. We never have attempted to withdraw the ones and twos from circulation.

Mr. PHILLIPS. But have they not gone out of circulation under the resumption act ?

Secretary SHERMAN. Not to any very great extent. They do not go out simply because the banks and others who draw large amounts do not take them as freely as the people wish to have them. The banks do not wish to handle them.

The CHAIRMAN. It seems to me that upon your theory, on resumption, it would be very important that greenbacks should be used for our four per cent. bonds ?

Secretary SHERMAN. Yes, sir.

The CHAIRMAN. And that if they can be also received for duties at the custom-house it would help you in resumption.

Secretary SHERMAN. Yes. As soon as we resume, or are ready to resume, we ought to receive greenbacks for customs-duties.

The CHAIRMAN. And bring them on a par with gold also by making them exchangeable for bonds.

Secretary SHERMAN. Yes; or redeem such as are presented in coin.

The CHAIRMAN. On that theory of resumption you would resume already, in order to have practical resumption.

Secretary SHERMAN. Yes; that is resumption, and we would not know about it. Within a year we have seen a decline of nine per cent. between greenbacks and gold. In December, 1876, gold was 110 per cent., and we have since had that decline and nobody has been hurt by it.

Mr. BELL. Suppose the greenbacks were to obtain an equality in value with gold, how would the repeal of the resumption act then affect resumption ?

Secretary SHERMAN. The repeal of the resumption act would prevent me from maintaining resumption by the sale of bonds. That would be the first thing. Then the resumption act is the only provision of law which requires me to redeem United States notes in coin.

Mr. EWING. But you are at liberty to do so. If the resumption act were repealed, you might maintain an equivalency of paper and coin ?

Secretary SHERMAN. No. It is perfectly clear that I have no right to exchange one form of money for another.

Mr. EWING. But you could pay out gold and silver.

Secretary SHERMAN. Yes.

Mr. EWING. And you could thus maintain an equality of coin and

---

* *Statement of one and two dollar United States notes outstanding at the dates mentioned.*

Date.	Ones.	Twos.	Totals.
June 30, 1873	28, 911, 309	34, 210, 856	63, 122, 165
June 30, 1874	26, 571, 512	28, 117, 438	54, 688, 950
June 30, 1875	27, 416, 863	26, 345, 326	53, 762, 189
June 30, 1866	28, 007, 504	27, 480, 479	55, 487, 983
June 30, 1877	25, 160, 297	25, 369, 825	50, 530, 122
April 1, 1878	22, 744, 288	22, 707, 443	45, 451, 731

paper upon your theory, which is, that as soon as paper and coin are equal nothing will be likely to occur to disturb the equilibrium?

Secretary SHERMAN. There will be more or less fluctuation, and we must be prepared to meet those fluctuations, so that if greenbacks become superabundant we can get gold for them; or if, on the other hand, gold becomes a drug, as it may, it will be deposited for greenbacks.

Mr. EWING. But if greenbacks become superabundant, and are presented to the Treasury for redemption, you will have to pay them out again?

Secretary SHERMAN. Yes, as soon as the equivalency is restored.

Mr. EWING. That is, you will hold whatever greenbacks come in until there is an equivalency?

Secretary SHERMAN. Yes; that is the effect of it.

Mr. PHILLIPS. Would it not be safer, by legislation and by taking greenbacks for customs-duties, to secure and maintain an equalization of values in that way rather than by resumption to authorize the combination of bankers to drain away the only credit resources in the Treasury?

Secretary SHERMAN. I think not; unless you maintain this equivalency you have no right, under your law, without violating your promise, to receive anything but coin in payment of customs-duties.

Mr. PHILLIPS. There may be various means of bringing up greenbacks by equalizing values. Would it not be safer for us to legislate so as to preserve an equality in values rather than to have forced resumption?

Secretary SHERMAN. No; because legislation is not powerful enough to do what can only be done by the actual redemption of the notes on presentation. No law can make two things equal to each other in values.

Mr. PHILLIPS. Can the law force you to resume if you have not the coin to do it?

Secretary SHERMAN. No; but we have the coin. As a matter of course, if we had not the coin we could not resume, but if we have the coin we can resume.

Mr. EWING. I understand that your idea is to exercise about the same power which is exercised by the Bank of England, in regard to these legal-tender notes.

Secretary SHERMAN. No; because the Bank of England loans out its notes for profit. That is its business.

Mr. EWING. The Bank of England, when a drain sets in, interrupts the movement of circulation by taking in its notes and not paying them out until the drain is checked. In that respect your idea of maintaining resumption is the same.

Secretary SHERMAN. Yes. When the notes are presented, the Secretary of the Treasury pays them in coin, silver or gold, at his discretion. When, in his judgment, it is wise to pay out these notes, either on the public debt or on the interest of the public debt, to those who are willing to take them, or any current expenses, he does it.

Mr. EWING. But he would not pay them out——

Secretary SHERMAN. Unless they were equivalent to coin.

Mr. EWING. And he would judge of their equivalency by the drain upon the Treasury?

Secretary SHERMAN. He would never be likely to pay out these greenbacks if they were to come back again on him for coin; and he would not be wise if he did it.

Mr. EWING. In that respect, he maintains resumption by exercising the same power and control over the paper currency as the Bank of England does?

Secretary SHERMAN. Yes, sir. Practically, that is done by the assistant treasurer in New York. I know, every day, how much coin-certificates are outstanding, and how much coin there is in the subtreasury. Every day these certificates are presented for redemption and somebody else deposits coin for other certificates, and thus the thing goes on, in ebb and flow, sometimes to the amount of a million or two a day. I see nothing of it, but I see the subtreasury reports every day. One man brings gold to the subtreasury and gets certificates, and another man brings the certificates and draws out the gold.

Mr. EWING. I think I have your idea pretty clearly that your control in putting out legal-tenders or withholding them is the lever by which their convertibility is to be maintained?

Secretary SHERMAN. Yes; and then there is, too, the fact that the Secretary is under the constant eye of Congress if he abuses his powers, because a great power is less liable to be abused than a small one. The eye of the public is on the Secretary in the exercise of power of this kind, and it is not likely to be abused. If there is any sign of his abusing it Congress is always present to prevent it. The Secretary would not dare to sell bonds to raise gold for resumption while he has any notes on hand unless there is a drain for the gold. All these powers will be exercised under the eye of Congress.

Mr. EWING. If there is a drain of gold you would sell bonds?

Secretary SHERMAN. The Secretary might sell bonds, and, again, when greenbacks were abundant in the Treasury he might make a call for six per cent. bonds, as I have done. I exercised my discretion in the matter last December, and I made a mistake in making a call for $10,000,000 of bonds which had better not have been made. I underestimated the effect of pending legislation. I did it under my discretion; but I did not sell enough bonds to redeem that call. So, the Secretary of the Treasury, administering under this law, if he found coin or greenbacks accumulating in his hands, would make a call of six per cent. bonds and would pay them off and sell four per cent. or four and a half per cent. bonds—whichever was the current bond in the market—and thus make good his money. That operation would go on without difficulty. That is the way, at least, that I would conduct it if I were in charge.

Mr. HARTZELL. I understood you to say that in order to complete your preparations for resumption additional bonds to the amount of, perhaps, fifty millions would have to be sold between now and the 1st of January.

Secretay SHERMAN. Yes; I think so.

Mr. HARTZELL. Is it your expectation that, after resumption day, you will have to continue the sale of bonds at different periods for the purpose of maintaining the specie reserve?

Secretary SHERMAN. Not at all. If I would sell any bonds at all after that, I would sell them merely for the purpose of refunding. It might be that, to meet a sudden drain, I would sell bonds in order to accumulate coin; but the very moment the drain ceased I would use the coin or the greenbacks which I had received in calling in 6 per cent bonds. Under that the whole of the public debt might be reduced to 4 per cents., if that should prove to be the ultimate rate of interest in this country.

Mr. HARTZELL. But the interest-bearing debt of the country has to be increased in order to bring about this result.

Secretary SHERMAN. Yes, in the absence of surplus revenue. There is no other way except by the increase of the public debt temporarily. We would have the coin to represent the bonds. That is all.

The conference here ended.

APPENDIX.

APPENDIX No. 1.

Statement of gold and silver in the Treasury on the 1st of February, 1877.

Gold coin	$71,944,129 47	
Gold bullion	8,720,150 25	
		$80,664,279 72
Less amount to credit of disbursing-officers, and outstanding checks	3,074,445 45	
Less gold certificates actually outstanding	50,791,240 00	
Less called bonds and interest	10,117,672 63	
Less interest due and unpaid	9,993,750 26	
		73,977,108 34
Available gold coin and bullion		$6,687,171 38
Silver coin	2,228,898 02	
Silver bullion	3,211,796 21	
	5,440,694 23	
Less outstanding checks	191,194 52	
Available silver coin and bullion		5,249,599 71
Available gold and silver coin and bullion		11,936,771 09

APPENDIX No. 2.

*Statement of coin and bullion in the Treasury February 1, 1878.**

Held by—	Gold coin.	Gold bullion.	Silver coin.	Silver bullion.
Treasurer United States, Washington ...	$397,628 39		$201,679 74	
Assistant treasurer United States, New York	92,024,604 20	$3,367,713 26	1,171,368 14	
Assistant treasurer United States, Boston	659,618 47		392,540 55	
Assistant treasurer United States, Philadelphia	454,884 35		809,674 75	
Assistant treasurer United States, Saint Louis	274,722 64		273,045 33	
Assistant treasurer United States, San Francisco	1,854,963 38		146,608 35	
Assistant treasurer United States, New Orleans	1,120,121 66		224,170 16	
Assistant treasurer United States, Baltimore	509,154 30		166,450 22	
Assistant treasurer United States, Cincinnati	280,064 83		217,877 33	
Assistant treasurer United States, Chicago	528,326 04		253,549 38	
Mint, Philadelphia	1,403,416 24	637,557 34	748,546 67	$671,116 55
Mint, San Francisco	978,757 74	5,039,352 92	41,327 65	893,651 51
Mint, Carson City	224,154 54	73,693 61	427,894 76	214,462 31
Mint, Denver	3,000 00		100 00	
United States assay-office, New York ...	3,672,671 37	2,079,834 24	21,148 22	1,048,137 70
United States assay-office, Boise City			500 00	
United States assay-office, Charlotte			200 00	
United States assay-office, Helena			500 00	
First National Bank, Milwaukee, Wis ...	28,078 19			
First National Bank, Portland, Oreg ...	165 00			
Totals	104,414,331 34	11,198,151 37	5,097,181 25	2,827,368 07

* The items to be deducted are the following, taken from page 4 of Senate interview :

Amount to credit of disbursing-officers and outstanding checks	$6,189,626 60
Gold-certificates actually outstanding	44,498,500 00
Called bonds and interest	6,818,677 29
Interest due and unpaid	4,909,705 21
	62,416,509 10

APPENDIX No. 3.

[In reply to inquiry No. 1. Letter of March 28, from Hon. A. H. Buckner.]

Statement of coin and bullion in Treasury at close of business February 28, 1878.

Held by—	Gold coin.	Gold bullion.	Silver coin.	Silver bullion.
Treasurer United States, Washington ..	$675, 899 51	....	$179, 377 97	....
Assistant treasurer United States, New York..........................	99, 899, 528 09	$3, 367, 713 26	1, 407, 992 53	....
Assistant treasurer United States, Boston	663, 577 50	....	379, 903 05	....
Assistant treasurer United States, Philadelphia...............................	467, 415 70	....	797, 294 75	....
Assistant treasurer United States, Saint Louis...............................	276, 031 00	....	263, 694 98	....
Assistant treasurer United States, San Francisco............................	2, 458, 100 00	....	149, 260 81	....
Assistant treasurer United States, New Orleans............................	1, 168, 719 00	....	217, 575 95	....
Assistant treasurer United States, Baltimore..................................	519, 301 50	....	157, 218 52	....
Assistant treasurer United States, Cincinnati..................................	251, 636 00	....	211, 828 16	....
Assistant treasurer United States, Chicago.....................................	665, 527 50	....	248, 319 12	....
Mint, Philadelphia	2, 829, 834 32	556, 035 45	887, 057 86	1, 244, 000 00
Mint, San Francisco.....................	4, 045, 079 73	1, 887, 305 36	72, 920 54	904, 861 65
Mint, Carson City........................	655, 147 80	46, 412 00	225, 145 33	175, 974 98
Mint, Denver	3, 000 00	....	100 00	....
United States assay-office, New York	3, 672, 671 37	2, 079, 834 24	21, 148 22	630, 741 02
United States assay-office, Boise City	....	....	500 00	....
United States assay-office, Charlotte	....	....	200 00	....
United States assay-office, Helena	....	....	500 00	....
National banks and depositaries	300, 150 03	....	456 45	....
In transit...................................	....	....	455, 000 00	....
Total	118, 351, 709 05	7, 937, 300 31	5, 675, 494 24	2, 955, 577 65

TREASURY UNITED STATES,
Washington, D. C., March 30, 1878.

APPENDIX No. 4.

Statement of coin and bullion in the Treasury March 28, 1878.

Date.	Offices, &c.	Gold coin and standard silver dollars.	Fractional silver coin.	Gold and silver bullion.
1878.				
March 27	Treasury of United States, Washington ..	$676, 282 68	$958, 165 65	....
27	Assistant treasury, Baltimore	511. 688 50	149, 093 52	....
27	Assistant treasury, New York	100, 128, 068 09	1, 374, 628 52	$3, 367, 713 26
27	Assistant treasury, Philadelphia..........	271, 109 97	791, 004 75	....
25	Assistant treasury, Boston.................	975, 607 50	370, 333 46	....
25	Assistant treasury, Cincinnati............	233, 659 50	207, 141 33	....
25	Assistant treasury, Chicago	623, 807 00	247, 819 89	....
25	Assistant treasury, Saint Louis...........	279, 373 00	251, 208 84	....
23	Assistant treasury, New Orleans	1, 139, 747 00	213, 706 76	....
19	Assistant treasury, San Francisco	2, 803, 900 00	150, 648 66	....
23	National bank depositories	2, 938, 910 93	....	....
23	Mint United States, Philadelphia	1, 245, 220 75	642, 114 97	1, 633, 609 46
16	Mint United States, San Francisco........	1, 903, 552 50	79, 260 86	4, 927, 353 92
9	Mint United States, Carson	933, 032 05	279, 260 09	65, 387 97
	Mint United States, Denver	3, 000 00	100 00	....
23	United States assay-office, New York.....	....	20, 951 89	3, 670, 849 85
	Other small assay-offices	....	1, 200 00	....
	Totals	114, 666, 958 97	5, 736, 639 19	13, 664, 914 46

NOTE.—Standard silver dollars included above, 454,711.

APPENDIX No. 5.

Comparison of condition of the Treasury April 1, 1877, and April 1, 1878.

Balances.	1877.	1878.
Currency	$8,184,863 58	$751,851 35
Special fund for the redemption of fractional currency		10,000,000,00
Special deposit of legal-tenders for redemption of certificates of deposit	35,155,000 00	25,215,000 00
Coin	86,818,285 26	138,357,608 14
Coin-certificates	48,279,400 00	57,883,400 00
Coin, less coin-certificates	38,538,885 26	80,474,208 14
Outstanding called bonds	5,262,900 00	7,305,200 00
Other outstanding coin liabilities	6,786,028 00	4,643,276 28
Outstanding legal-tenders	362,656,204 00	347,848,712 00
Outstanding fractional currency	23,440,512 08	16,950,115 62
Outstanding silver coin	29,937,001 43	38,662,487 02
Total debt, less cash in Treasury	2,074,674,126 63	2,039,723,514 31
Reduction of debt for March	*14,107,016 41	2,313,614 77
Reduction of debt since July 1	*24,765,218 36	20,434,708 95
Market value of gold	105 00	101 25
Imports (12 months ending February 28)	420,199,831 00	475,638,634 00
Exports (12 months ending February 28)	603,631,538 00	637,757,892 00

* This reduction includes $9,553,800 Geneva award bonds canceled.

TREASURY DEPARTMENT, WARRANT DIVISION.

APPENDIX No. 6.

Circulation and deposits, and specie of the State banks, 1857 and 1860.

Years.	Circulation.	Deposits and bank balances.	Total.	Specie.	Ratios of specie to—	
					Circulation.	Circulation and deposits.
					Per cent.	Per cent.
1857	$214,778,822	$230,351,352	$445,130,174	$58,349,838	27.2	13.1
1860	207,102,477	253,802,129	460,904,606	83,594,537	40.4	18.1

Compiled from statement in Finance Report, 1876, pages 204, 205.

Circulation, deposits, and cash reserve of the national banks, December 28, 1877.

LIABILITIES.

Circulation	$299,240,475
Deposits	661,575,577
Total	960,816,052

CASH RESERVE HELD.

Gold coin	$5,506,556	
Silver coin	4,300,274	
United States gold-certificates	23,100,920	
Total specie		32,907,750
Legal-tender notes	$70,568,248	
United States certificates for legal-tenders	26,515,000	
Total legal-tenders		97,083,248
Five per cent. redemption fund		15,028,340
Total cash reserve		145,019,338

Ratio of legal-tender funds to circulation	48.4 per cent.
Ratio of legal-tender funds to circulation and deposits	15.1 per cent.

Circulation, deposits, and cash resources of the national banks December 28, 1877.

LIABILITIES.

Circulation	$299, 240, 475
Deposits	661, 575, 577
Total	960, 816, 052

CASH RESOURCES.

Gold coin	$5, 506, 556	
Silver coin	4, 300, 274	
United States gold-certificates	23, 100, 920	
Total specie		32, 907, 750
Legal tender-notes	$70, 568, 248	
United States certificates for legal-tenders	26, 515, 000	
Total legal-tenders		97, 083, 248
Five per cent. redemption fund		15, 028, 340
United States bonds, par value, $285,887,350; currency value, $405,181,717		405, 161, 717
Total cash resources		550, 201, 035
Ratio of cash resources to circulation		183 + per cent.
Ratio of cash resources to circulation and deposits		57.3 per cent.

Abstract of reports made to the Comptroller of the Currency, showing the condition of the national banks in the United States, including national gold banks, at the close of business on Friday, the 28th day of December, 1877.

Resources.		Liabilities.	
Loans and discounts	$878, 055, 305 95	Capital stock paid in	$447, 128, 771 00
Overdrafts	3, 801, 438 92		
United States bonds to secure circulation.	343, 869, 550 00	Surplus fund	121, 618, 455 32
United States bonds to secure deposits..	13, 538, 000 00	Other undivided profits..	51, 530, 910 18
United States bonds on hand	28, 479, 800 00		
Other stocks, bonds, and mortgages	39, 189, 491 03	National bank notes outstanding*	299, 240, 475 00
Due from approved reserve agents	75, 960, 087 27		
Due from other national banks	44, 123, 924 97	State bank notes outstanding	470, 540 00
Due from State banks and bankers	11, 479, 945 65		
Real estate, furniture, and fixtures	45, 511, 932 25		
Current expenses	8, 958, 903 60	Dividends unpaid	1, 404, 178 34
Premiums paid	8, 841, 939 09		
Checks and other cash items	10, 265, 059 49	Individual deposits	604, 512, 514 52
Exchanges for clearing-house	64, 664, 415 01	United States deposits...	6, 529, 031 09
Bills of other national banks	20, 312, 692 00	Deposits of United States	
Fractional currency	778, 084 78	disbursing officers	3, 780, 759 43
Specie, viz:			
Gold coin $5,506.556.39		Due to other national	
Silver coin 4,300,274.31	32, 907, 750 70	banks	115, 773, 660 58
U. S. gold certificates. 23,100,920.00		Due to State banks and	
Legal-tender notes	70, 568, 248 00	bankers	44, 807, 958 79
United States certificates of deposit for legal-tender notes	26, 515, 000 00	Notes and bills rediscounted	4, 654, 784 51
Five per cent. redemption fund with Treasurer	15, 028, 340 14	Bills payable	5, 843, 107 03
Due from Treasurer other than redemption fund	1, 465, 236 94		
Aggregate	1, 737, 295, 145 79	**Aggregate**	1,737,295, 145 79

* The amount of circulation outstanding at the date named, as shown by the books of this office, was $321,672,505; which amount includes the notes of insolvent banks, of those in voluntary liquidation, and of those which have deposited legal-tender notes under the act of June 20, 1874, for the purpose of retiring their circulation.

JNO. JAY KNOX,
Comptroller of the Currency.

TREASURY DEPARTMENT,
OFFICE COMPTROLLER OF THE CURRENCY,
Washington, February 16, 1878.

APPENDIX No. 7.

Statement showing the apparent and probable condition of the United States Treasury, including the proposed accumulation of $50,000,000 coin.

	Apparent.	Probable.
Demand liabilities, April 1, 1878:		
Legal-tender notes	$347, 848, 712 00	$340, 000, 000 00
Coin-certificates	57, 883, 400 00	57, 883, 400 00
Interest overdue	4, 121, 146 77	4, 000, 000 00
Debt, matured and interest	8, 439, 391 04	8, 000, 000 00
Currency-certificates	25, 215, 000 00	25, 215, 000 00
Fractional currency	16, 950, 115 62	
Demand notes	62, 342 50	
Unclaimed Pacific Railroad interest	7, 267 03	
Totals	460, 527, 374 96	435, 098, 400 00
Demand resources, April 1, 1878:		
Coin	138, 357, 608 14	188, 357, 608 14
Currency	35, 966, 851 35	35, 966, 851 35
Totals	174, 324, 459 49	224, 324, 459 49
Percentage of resources to liabilities	. 37	. 51

APPENDIX No. 8.

Statement showing resources and liabilities of certain European banks at dates mentioned below.

Bank.	Date.	Demand liabilities. Circulation.	Demand liabilities. Deposits.	Total.	Demand resources. Bullion.	Percentage of resources to liabilities.	Average depreciation, per cent.
Bank of England	1818	26, 202, 000	7, 928, 000	34, 130, 000	6, 363, 000	.18+	2. 13. 2.
Do	1820	24, 299, 000	4, 421, 000	28, 720, 000	8, 211, 000	.28+	2. 12. 0.
Do	1822	17, 465, 000	6, 399, 000	23, 864, 000	10, 098, 000	.42+	Nil.
Do	1824	20, 132, 000	9, 680, 000	29, 812, 000	11, 787, 000	.39+	Nil.
Do	1826	21, 564, 000	7, 200, 000	28, 764, 000	6, 754, 000	.23+	Nil.
Do	1828	21, 358, 000	10, 201, 000	31, 559, 000	10, 499, 000	.33+	Nil.
Do	1830	21, 465, 000	11, 621, 000	33, 086, 000	11, 150, 000	.33+	Nil.
Do	1832	18, 320, 000	10, 278, 000	28, 598, 000	7, 514, 000	.26+	Nil.
Do	1834	19, 195, 000	13, 300, 000	32, 495, 000	7, 303, 000	.22+	Nil.
Do	1836	18, 018, 000	12, 040, 000	30, 058, 000	5, 250, 000	.17+	Nil.
Do	1838	19, 488, 000	8, 922, 000	28, 410, 000	9, 540, 000	.33+	Nil.
Do	1840	17, 170, 000	6, 254, 000	23, 424, 000	4, 299, 000	.18+	Nil
Do	1842	20, 332, 000	8, 690, 000	29, 022, 000	9, 729, 000	.33+	Nil.
Do	1844	21, 485, 000	12, 138, 000	33, 623, 000	15, 315, 000	.45+	Nil.
Do	1846	21, 390, 000	16, 322, 000	37, 712, 000	16, 388, 000	.43+	Nil.
Do	1878. Feb. 20	26, 584, 674	28, 054, 497	54, 639, 171	24, 730, 793	.45+	Nil
Bank of France	Feb. 14	99, 350, 000	21, 193, 000	120, 543, 000	78, 896, 000	.65+	
Bank of Germany	Feb. 7	30, 987, 000	10, 311, 000	41, 298, 000	24, 759, 000	.58+	
National Bank of Belgium	Feb. 7	13, 170, 000	2, 330, 000	15, 500, 000	3, 991, 000	.25+	

APPENDIX No. 9.

An estimate of the amount of gold and silver bullion and coin in the United States April 1, 1878.

Gold.

In United States Treasury (including bullion fund of mints and assay office) October 31, 1877	$125, 122, 843 94
In national banks (exclusive of coin-certificates) October 1, 1877	4, 867, 909 18
In California banks	18, 000, 000 00
Private banks (Pacific coast)	2, 000, 000 00
State and county treasuries (Pacific coast)	4, 000, 000 00

Merchants and individuals (Pacific coast)..............	84,000,000 00
Unpaid deposits, United States mints.............. .	500,000 00
Smelters and private refiners (exclusive of the Pacific coast)..	500,000 00
Gold bullion in California............................	1,500,000 00
In private hands, including bullion dealers, savings-banks, and private bankers east of the Rocky Mountains...	15,000,000 00
In State banks.......................................	2,000,000 00

	177,490,753 12
Production from October 31 to April 1..............	20,000,000 00
Approximate excess of imports over exports	2,000,000 00

	199,490,753 12

Silver.

Fractional coin in States east of the Rocky Mountains, including trade-dollars and Mexican coin, October 31, 1877.	842,000,000
California banks ....:..............................	2,000,000
Private banks (Pacific coast)............................	500,000
State and county treasuries (Pacific coast)	500,000
Merchants and individuals (Pacific coast)...................	500,000
Silver bullion (Pacific coast)...........	2,000,000
Silver bullion in hands of smelters and refiners east of the Rocky Mountains	1,000,000

	48,500,000
Silver bullion in mints	2,000,000
Production from mines to April 1	15,000,000

	65,500,000

I have not the data necessary to ascertain to which of the foregoing items should be credited the gain of gold and silver since October 31, 1877. It may be stated, however, that the Treasury stock has been increased, and the amount of trade and Mexican dollars which have gone into circulation may be set down at not less than 4,000,000, exclusive of about 1,200,000 trade-dollars in the mints.

According to the above estimate the amount of gold coin and bullion now in the country is	8199,490,753 12
And silver coin and bullion	65,500,000 00

Total	264,990,753 12

Allowing for gold and silver used in the arts and for manufacturing purposes and possible overestimation, say $15,000,000, the total amount of gold and silver in the country may be set down at about two hundred and fifty millions of dollars, of which about fifty millions are in the form of fractional silver, trade dollars, and Mexican coin, and $1,200,000 in standard silver dollars.

THE PRESENT AVERAGE PRODUCTION OF GOLD AND SILVER FROM THE MINES OF THE UNITED STATES.

I have availed myself of every facility to procure full information in relation to the product of the gold and silver mines of the United States, for the purpose of estimating approximately the present annual yield, with the following results, based upon the production for the first six months of the year and the average monthly out-turn since, so far as it was possible to ascertain the same:

State or Territory.	Gold.	Silver.	Total.
California	$15, 000, 000	$1, 000, 000	$16, 000, 01 0
Nevada	18, 000, 000	26, 000, 000	44, 000, 000
Montana	3, 200, 000	750, 000	3, 950, 0C0
Idaho	1, 500, 000	250, 000	1, 750, 000
Utah	350, 000	5, 075, 000	5, 425, 000
Colorado	3, 000, 000	4, 500, 000	7, 500, 000
Arizona	300, 000	500, 000	800, 000
New Mexico	175, 000	500, 000	675, 000
Oregon	1, 000, 000	100, 000	1, 100, 000
Washington	300, 000	50, 000	350, 000
Dakota	2, 000, 000	....	2, 000, 000
Lake Superior	....	200, 000	200, 000
Virginia	50, 000	....	50, 000
North Carolina	100, 000	....	100, 000
Georgia	100, 000	....	100, 000
Other sources	25, 000	25, 000	50, 000
Total	45, 100, 000	38, 950, 000	84, 050, 000

It is impossible to state with any degree of accuracy how long this large rate of production will be maintained. A gradual increase may be expected in Montana and Arizona, and there is nothing to indicate a decrease in any bullion-producing State or Territory, except in the State of Nevada, and that depends upon contingencies which to a great extent must be a matter of conjecture only. Several mines in different localities in that State have within the last year or two been opened and are producing considerable bullion, but whether they, and others which in the mean time may be discovered, will yield sufficient to make up the decrease, which, unless other ore-bodies on the Comstock shall be found, must sooner or later take place, is somewhat doubtful.

The superintendent of the mint at San Francisco has furnished, at my request, a statement, embraced in the appendix, of the yield of about thirty different mines, the bullion from which finds a market in San Francisco.

The yield of bullion from the two mines which embrace the great ore-chimney discovered in 1874 in the Comstock lode has, according to the official statement of the managers, amounted, up to October 31, 1877, to $78,852,918.48, of which $36,736,347.91 was gold. These mines are now producing at the rate of nearly three million dollars per month.

H. R. LINDERMAN,
Director of the Mint.

TREASURY DEPARTMENT, April 3, 1878.

APPENDIY No. 10.

Statement of imports and exports of specie (coin and bullion) during the fiscal years ended June 30, 1865, to 1877, inclusive, and the seven months ended January 31, 1878.

Fiscal years ended June 30—	Coin and bullion.					
	Exports.			Imports.	Excess of—	
	Domestic.	Foreign.	Total.		Imports.	Exports.
1865.........................	$64, 618, 124	$3, 025, 102	$67, 643, 226	$9, 810, 072	....	$57, 833, 154
1866.........................	82, 643, 374	3, 400, 697	86, 044, 071	10, 700, 092	....	75, 343, 979
1867.........................	54, 976, 196	5, 892, 176	60, 868, 372	22, 070, 475	....	38, 797, 897
1868.........................	83, 715, 975	10, 038, 127	93, 784, 102	14, 188, 368	....	79, 595, 734
1869.........................	42, 915, 966	14, 222, 414	57, 138, 380	19, 807, 876	....	37, 330, 504
1870.........................	43, 883, 802	14, 271, 864	58, 155, 666	26, 419, 179	....	31, 736, 487
1871.........................	84, 403, 359	14, 038, 629	98, 441, 988	21, 270, 024	....	77, 171, 964
1872.........................	72, 798, 240	7, 079, 294	79, 877, 534	13, 743, 689	....	66, 133, 845
1873	73, 905, 546	10, 703, 028	84, 608, 574	21, 480, 937	....	63, 127, 637
1874.........................	59, 699, 686	6, 930, 719	66, 630, 405	28, 454, 906	....	38, 175, 499
1875.........................	83, 857, 129	8, 275, 013	92, 132, 142	20, 900, 717	....	71, 231, 425
1876.........................	50, 038, 691	6, 467, 611	56, 506, 302	15, 936, 681	....	40, 569, 621
1877.........................	43, 134, 738	13, 027, 499	56, 162, 237	40, 774, 414	....	15, 387, 823
1877.						
July	4, 197, 923	285, 641	4, 483, 564	1, 107, 814	....	3, 375, 750
August	1, 665, 357	388, 596	2, 053, 883	1, 642, 143	....	411, 740
September	2, 239, 416	844, 195	3, 083, 611	3, 840, 382	$756, 771	....
October......................	1, 693, 583	317, 379	2, 010, 962	1, 717, 793	....	293, 169
November	1, 197, 733	367, 121	1, 564, 854	2, 266, 083	701, 229	....
December	1, 539, 446	380, 451	1, 919, 897	1, 670, 265	....	249, 632
1878.						
January	3, 230, 996	522, 758	3, 753, 754	1, 790, 964	....	1, 962, 790

Total for years 1865 to 1877, inclusive	$692, 435, 569
Average..	53, 264, 000
Average for last three years	42, 396, 000
Average gold and silver product of the United States, 1870 to 1876, inclusive..............	71, 000, 000
Average excess of production over net export, 1874, 1875, and 1876, $29,000,000 ; deduct $7,000,000 used in arts ; leaving...	22, 000, 000

EDWARD YOUNG,
Chief of Bureau.

BUREAU OF STATISTICS, *March* 29, 1878.

Hon. THOMAS EWING, *M. C.*

APPENDIX No. 11.

Distribution of currency in the Treasury of the United States, March 28, 1878.

Date.	Office, &c.	United States notes.	National-bank notes.	Currency.
1878.				
March 27	Treasurer United States, Washington...........	$6, 432, 588 20	$122, 261 50	....
27	Assistant treasurer United States, New York...	32, 107, 136 84	468, 066 92	....
27	Assistant treasurer United States, Baltimore ...	3, 481, 053 00	44, 478 00	....
27	Assistant treasurer United States, Philadelphia	4, 730, 620 00	38, 800 00	....
25	Assistant treasurer United States, Boston	3, 608, 000 00	206, 836 00	....
25	Assistant treasurer United States, Cincinnati...	1, 322, 089 00	356, 000 00	....
25	Assistant treasurer United States, Chicago......	3, 629, 500 00	356, 785 00	....
25	Assistant treasurer United States, Saint Louis..	2, 270, 094 00	....	....
23	Assistant treasurer United States, New Orleans.	1, 560, 000 00	163, 000 00	....
19	Assistant treasurer United States, San Francisco	1, 127, 300 00	470, 000 00	....
9	Depositary United States, Tucson...............	370, 610 00	....	....
	National-bank depositaries......................	....	....	$6, 065, 059 69
23	Mint United States, Philadelphia	90, 538 00	....	....
	Total.......................	60, 729, 529 04	2, 246, 227 42	6, 065, 059 69

APPENDIX No. 12.

[From Dr. Linderman's official report.]

Annual product of gold and silver from the American mines.

Year.	Gold.	Silver.	Total.
1870	$50,000,000	$16,000,000	$66,000,000
1871	43,500,000	23,000,000	66,500,000
1872	36,000,000	28,750,000	64,750,000
1873	36,000,000	35,750,000	71,750,000
1874	40,000,000	32,000,000	72,000,000
1875	40,000,000	32,000,000	72,000,000
1876	44,300,000	41,500,000	85,700,000
1877 (Wells, Fargo & Co.'s estimate)	....	....	100,000,000

Exports of specie in the fiscal years 1872, 1873, and 1874, in excess of imports for same years $167,436,981
Average for each year... 55,812,000
Excess of exports for the years 1875, 1876, and 1877....................................... 127,188,797
Average for each year... 42,396,000
Excess since July 1, 1877, to January 31, 1878, inclusive.................................... 4,835,041

INDEX.

○